Maple 8
Learning Guide

Based in part on the work of B. W. Char

with 10 color figures

Waterloo Maple Inc.
57 Erb Street West
Waterloo, ON N2L 6C2
Canada

Contents

1   Introduction to Maple

Maple is a *Symbolic Computation System* or *Computer Algebra System*. Maple manipulates information in a symbolic or algebraic manner. Other conventional mathematical programs require numerical values for all variables. In contrast, Maple maintains and manipulates the underlying symbols and expressions, and evaluates numerical expressions.

You can use these symbolic capabilities to obtain exact analytical solutions to many mathematical problems, including integrals, systems of equations, differential equations, and problems in linear algebra. Complementing the symbolic operations are a large set of graphics routines for visualizing complicated mathematical information, numerical algorithms for providing estimates and solving problems where exact solutions do not exist, and a complete and comprehensive programming language for developing custom functions and applications.

Maple's extensive mathematical functionality is most easily accessed through its advanced worksheet-based graphical interface. A worksheet is a flexible document for exploring mathematical ideas and for creating sophisticated technical reports. Users of Maple have found countless ways to utilize the Maple language and worksheets.

Engineers and professionals in industries as diverse as agriculture and aerospace use Maple as a productivity tool, replacing many traditional resources such as reference books, calculators, spreadsheets, and programming languages such as FORTRAN. These users easily produce answers to a wide range of day-to-day mathematical problems, creating projections and consolidating their computations into professional technical reports.

Researchers in many fields find Maple to be an essential tool for their work. Maple is ideal for formulating, solving, and exploring mathematical models. Its symbolic manipulation facilities greatly extend the range of problems you can solve.

Instructors use Maple to present lectures. Educators in high schools, colleges, and universities have revitalized traditional curricula by introducing problems and exercises that use Maple's interactive mathematics. Students can concentrate on important concepts, rather than tedious algebraic manipulations.

The way in which you use Maple is in some aspects personal and dependent on your needs, but two modes are particularly prevalent.

The first mode is as an interactive problem-solving environment. When you work on a problem in a traditional manner, attempting a particular solution method can take hours and many pages of paper. Maple allows you to undertake much larger problems and eliminates your mechanical errors. The interface provides documentation of the steps involved in finding your result. It allows you to easily modify a step or insert a new one in your solution method. With minimal effort you can compute the new result. Whether you are developing a new mathematical model or analyzing a financial strategy, you can learn a great deal about the problem easily and efficiently.

The second mode in which you can use Maple is as a system for generating technical documents. You can create interactive structured documents that contain mathematics in which you can change an equation and update the solution automatically. Maple's natural mathematical language allows easy entry of equations. You also can compute and display plots. In addition, you can structure your documents by using modern tools such as styles, outlining, and hyperlinks, creating documents that are not only clear and easy to use, but easy to maintain. Since components of worksheets are directly associated with the structure of the document, you can easily translate your work to other formats, such as HTML, RTF, LaTeX, and XML.

Many types of documents can benefit from the features of Maple's worksheets. These facilities save you a great deal of effort if you are writing a report or a mathematical book. They are also appropriate for creating and displaying presentations and lectures. For example, outlining allows you to collapse sections to hide regions that contain distracting detail. Styles identify keywords and headings. Hyperlinks allow you to create live references that take the reader directly to pages containing related information. Above all, the interactive nature of Maple allows you to compute results and answer questions during presentations. You can clearly and effectively demonstrate why a seemingly acceptable solution method is inappropriate, or why a particular modification to a manufacturing process would lead to loss or profit.

This book is your introduction to Maple. It systematically discusses important concepts and builds a framework of knowledge that guides you in your use of the interface and the Maple language. This manual provides an overview of the functionality of Maple. It describes both the symbolic and numeric capabilities, introducing the available Maple objects, commands, and methods. Particular emphasis is placed on not only finding solutions, but also plotting or animating results and exporting worksheets to other formats. More importantly, it presents the philosophy and methods of use intended by the designers of the system. These simple concepts allow you to use Maple fully and efficiently.

Whereas this book is a guide that highlights features of Maple, the online help system is a complete reference manual. The Maple help system is more convenient than a traditional text because it allows you to search in many ways and is always available. There are also examples that you can copy, paste, and execute immediately.

1.1   Manual Set

There are three other manuals available for Maple, the *Maple 8 Getting Started Guide*, the *Maple 8 Introductory Programming Guide*, and the *Maple 8 Advanced Programming Guide*.[1]

The *Maple Getting Started Guide* contains an introduction to the graphical user interface and a tutorial that outlines using Maple to solve mathematical problems and create technical documents. In it, there is additional information for new users about the online help system, New User's Tour, example worksheets, and Waterloo Maple Web site.

The *Maple Introductory Programming Guide* introduces the basic Maple programming concepts, such as expressions, data structures, looping and decisions mechanisms, procedures, input and output, debugging, and `Maplets`.

The *Maple Advanced Programming Guide* extends the basic Maple programming concepts to more advanced topics, such as modules, input and output, numerical programming, graphics programming, and compiled code.

---

[1] The Student Edition does not include the *Maple 8 Introductory Programming Guide* and the *Maple 8 Advanced Programming Guide*. These programming guides can be purchased from school and speciality bookstores or directly from Waterloo Maple Inc.

2 Mathematics with Maple: the Basics

This chapter begins with a discussion of exact numeric calculations in Maple, which differ slightly from most other mathematical applications. Basic symbolic computations and assignment statements follow. The final two sections teach the basic types of objects in Maple, and provide an introduction to the manipulation of objects and the commands most useful for this purpose.

You will learn the most from this book by using your computer to try the examples as you read. This chapter sketches out the Maple commands necessary to get you started. Subsequent chapters give these and other commands a more in-depth treatment.

To develop a deeper understanding of Maple, use the online help facility. To use the help command, at the Maple prompt enter a question mark (?) followed by the name of the command or topic for which you want more information.

```
?command
```

2.1 Introduction

The most basic computations in Maple are numeric. Maple can function as a conventional calculator with integers or floating-point numbers. Enter the expression using natural syntax. A semicolon (;) marks the end of each calculation. Press ENTER to perform the calculation.

```
>  1 + 2;
```

3

```
> 1 + 3/2;
```

$$\frac{5}{2}$$

```
> 2*(3+1/3)/(5/3-4/5);
```

$$\frac{100}{13}$$

```
> 2.8754/2;
```

$$1.437700000$$

Consider a simple example.

```
> 1 + 1/2;
```

$$\frac{3}{2}$$

Note that Maple computes exact calculations with rational numbers. The result of $1 + 1/2$ is $3/2$ not 1.5. To Maple, the rational number $3/2$ and the floating-point approximation 1.5 are distinct objects. The ability to represent exact expressions allows Maple to preserve much more information about their origins and structure. The origin and structure of a number such as

$$0.5235987758$$

are much less clear than for an exact quantity such as

$$\frac{1}{6}\pi$$

When you begin to deal with more complex expressions the advantage is greater still.

Maple can work with rational numbers and arbitrary expressions. It can manipulate integers, floating-point numbers, variables, sets, sequences, polynomials over a ring, and many more mathematical constructs. In addition, Maple is also a complete programming language that contains procedures, tables, and other programming constructs.

2.2   Numerical Computations

Integer Computations

Integer calculations are straightforward. Remember to terminate each command with a semicolon.

```
> 1 + 2;
```

$$3$$

```
> 75 - 3;
```

$$72$$

```
> 5*3;
```

$$15$$

```
> 120/2;
```

$$60$$

Maple can also work with arbitrarily large integers. The practical limit on integers is approximately 2^{28} digits, depending mainly on the speed and resources of your computer. Maple can calculate large integers, count the number of digits in a number, and factor integers. For numbers, or other types of continuous output, that span more than one line on the screen, Maple uses the continuation character (\) to indicate that the output is continuous. That is, the backslash and following line ending should be ignored.

```
> 100!;
```

$$93326215443944152681699238856266700490 7\backslash$$
$$15968264381621468592963895217599993229\backslash$$
$$91560894146397615651828625369792082722\backslash$$
$$37582511852109168640000000000000000000\backslash$$
$$00000$$

```
> length(%);
```

158

This answer indicates the number of digits in the last example. The ditto operator, (%), is simply a shorthand reference to the result of the previous computation. To recall the second- or third-most previous computation result, use %% and %%%, respectively.

> ifactor(60);

$$(2)^2 \ (3) \ (5)$$

In addition to ifactor, Maple has many commands for working with integers, some of which allow for calculations of a greatest common divisor (gcd) of two integers, integer quotients and remainders, and primality tests. See the following examples, as well as Table 2.1.

> igcd(123, 45);

$$3$$

> iquo(25,3);

$$8$$

> isprime(18002676583);

$$true$$

Exact Arithmetic—Rationals, Irrationals, and Constants

An important Maple property is the ability to perform exact rational arithmetic, that is, to work with rational numbers (fractions) without reducing them to floating-point approximations.

> 1/2 + 1/3;

$$\frac{5}{6}$$

Maple handles the rational numbers and produces an exact result. The distinction between *exact* and *approximate* results is an important

Table 2.1 Commands for Working with Integers

Function	*Description*
abs	absolute value of an expression
factorial	factorial of an integer
iquo	quotient of an integer division
irem	remainder of an integer division
iroot	approximate integer root of an integer
isqrt	approximate integer square root of an integer
max, min	maximum and minimum of a set of inputs
mod	modular arithmetic
surd	real root of an integer

one. The ability to perform exact computations with computers enables you to solve a range of problems.

Maple can produce floating-point estimates. Maple can work with floating-point numbers with many thousands of digits, producing accurate estimates of exact expressions.

```
> Pi;
```

$$\pi$$

```
> evalf(Pi, 100);
```

$$3.141592653589793238462643383279502884197169399375105820974944592307816406286\backslash$$
$$20899862803482534211 7068$$

Learning how Maple distinguishes between exact and floating-point representations of values is important.

Here is an example of a rational (exact) number.

```
> 1/3;
```

$$\frac{1}{3}$$

The following is its floating-point approximation (shown to ten digits, by default).

> evalf(%);

$$0.3333333333$$

These results are not the same mathematically, nor are they at all the same in Maple.

Whenever you enter a number in decimal form, Maple treats it as a floating-point approximation. The presence of a decimal number in an expression causes Maple to produce an approximate floating-point result, since it cannot produce an exact solution from approximate data.

> 3/2*5;

$$\frac{15}{2}$$

> 1.5*5;

$$7.5$$

Thus, you should *use floating-point numbers only when you want to restrict Maple to working with non-exact expressions.*

You can enter exact quantities by using symbolic representation, like π, in contrast to 3.14. Maple interprets irrational numbers as exact quantities. Here is how you represent the square root of two in Maple.

> sqrt(2);

$$\sqrt{2}$$

Here is another square root example.

> sqrt(3)^2;

$$3$$

Maple recognizes the standard mathematical constants, such as π and the base of the natural logarithms, e. It works with them as exact quantities.

> Pi;

$$\pi$$

```
> sin(Pi);
```

$$0$$

The exponential function is represented by the Maple function `exp`.

```
> exp(1);
```

$$e$$

```
> ln(exp(5));
```

$$5$$

Actually, the example with π may look confusing. Remember that when Maple is producing typeset real-math notation, that is, it attempts to represent mathematical expressions as you might write them yourself. Thus, you enter π as `Pi` and Maple displays it as π.

Maple is case sensitive, so ensure that you use proper capitalization when stating these constants. The names `Pi`, `pi`, and `PI` are distinct. The names `pi` and `PI` are used to display the lower case and upper case Greek letters π and Π, respectively. For more information on Maple constants, enter `?constants` at the Maple prompt.

Floating-Point Approximations

Maple works with exact values, but it can return a floating-point approximation up to about 2^{28} digits, depending upon your computer's resources.

Ten or twenty accurate digits in floating-point numbers may seem adequate for almost any purpose, but two problems, in particular, severely limit the usefulness of such a system.

First, when subtracting two floating-point numbers of almost equal magnitude, the difference's relative error may be very large. This is known as *catastrophic cancellation*. For example, if two numbers are identical in their first seventeen (of twenty) digits, their difference is a three-digit number accurate to only three digits! In this case, you would need to use almost forty digits to produce twenty accurate digits in the answer.

Second, a result's mathematical form is more concise, compact, and convenient than its numerical value. For instance, an exponential function provides more information about the nature of a phenomenon than a large set of numbers with twenty accurate digits. An exact analytical description can also determine the behavior of a function when extrapolating to regions for which no data exists.

The `evalf` command converts an exact numerical expression to a floating-point number.

```
> evalf(Pi);
```

$$3.141592654$$

By default, Maple calculates the result using ten digits of accuracy, but you can specify any number of digits. Simply indicate the number after the numerical expression, using the following notation.

```
> evalf(Pi, 200);
```

$$
\begin{aligned}
&3.1415926535897932384626433832795028841\backslash \\
&9716939937510582097494459230781640628 6\backslash \\
&2089986280348253421170679821480865132 8\backslash \\
&2306647093844609550582231725359408128 4\backslash \\
&8111745028410270193852110555964462294 8\backslash \\
&9549303820
\end{aligned}
$$

You can also force Maple to do all its computations with floating-point approximations by including at least one floating-point number in each expression. Floats are "contagious": if an expression contains even one floating-point number, Maple evaluates the entire expression using floating-point arithmetic.

```
> 1/3 + 1/4 + 1/5.3;
```

$$0.7720125786$$

```
> sin(0.2);
```

$$0.1986693308$$

While the optional second argument to `evalf` controls the number of floating-point digits for that particular calculation, the special variable `Digits` sets the number of floating-point digits for all subsequent calculations.

```
> Digits := 20;
```

$$Digits := 20$$

```
> sin(0.2);
```

$$0.19866933079506121546$$

`Digits` is now set to twenty, which Maple then uses at each step in a calculation. Maple works like a calculator or an ordinary computer application in this respect. Remember that when you evaluate a complicated numerical expression, errors can accumulate to reduce the accuracy of the result to less than twenty digits. In general, setting `Digits` to produce a given accuracy is not easy, as the final result depends on your particular question. Using larger values, however, usually gives you some indication. If required, Maple can provide extreme floating-point accuracy.

Arithmetic with Special Numbers

Maple can work with complex numbers. I is Maple's default symbol for the square root of minus one, that is, $I = \sqrt{-1}$.

```
> (2 + 5*I) + (1 - I);
```

$$3 + 4I$$

```
> (1 + I)/(3 - 2*I);
```

$$\frac{1}{13} + \frac{5}{13}I$$

You can also work with other bases and number systems.

```
> convert(247, binary);
```

$$11110111$$

```
> convert(1023, hex);
```

$$3FF$$

```
> convert(17, base, 3);
```

$$[2,\,2,\,1]$$

Maple returns an integer base conversion as a list of digits; otherwise, a line of numbers, like 221, may be ambiguous, especially when dealing with large bases. Note that Maple lists the digits in order from least significant to most significant.

Maple also supports arithmetic in finite rings and fields.

```
> 27 mod 4;
```

$$3$$

Symmetric and positive representations are both available.

```
> mods(27,4);
```

$$-1$$

```
> modp(27,4);
```

$$3$$

The default for the mod command is positive representation, but you can change this option (for details, refer to ?mod).

Maple can also work with Gaussian Integers. The GaussInt package has about thirty commands for working with these special numbers. Enter ?GaussInt at the Maple prompt for more information about these commands.

Mathematical Functions

Maple contains all the standard mathematical functions (see Table 2.2 for a partial list).

```
> sin(Pi/4);
```

$$\frac{1}{2}\sqrt{2}$$

```
> ln(1);
```

Table 2.2 Select Mathematical Functions in Maple

Function	*Description*
sin, cos, tan, etc.	trigonometric functions
sinh, cosh, tanh, etc.	hyperbolic trigonometric functions
arcsin, arccos, arctan, etc.	inverse trigonometric functions
exp	exponential function
ln	natural logarithmic function
log[10]	logarithmic function base 10
sqrt	algebraic square root function
round	round to the nearest integer
trunc	truncate to the integer part
frac	fractional part
BesselI, BesselJ, BesselK, BesselY	Bessel functions
binomial	binomial function
erf, erfc	error & complementary error functions
Heaviside	Heaviside step function
Dirac	Dirac delta function
MeijerG	Meijer G function
Zeta	Riemann Zeta function
LegendreKc, LegendreKc1, LegendreEc, LegendreEc1, LegendrePic, LegendrePic1	Legendre's elliptic integrals
hypergeom	hypergeometric function

$$0$$

When Maple cannot find a simpler form, it leaves the expression as it is rather than convert it to an inexact form.

```
> ln(Pi);
```

$$\ln(\pi)$$

2.3   Basic Symbolic Computations

Maple can work with mathematical unknowns, and expressions which contain them.

```
> (1 + x)^2;
```

$$(1+x)^2$$

```
> (1 + x) + (3 - 2*x);
```

$$4 - x$$

Note that Maple automatically simplifies the second expression.

Maple has hundreds of commands for working with symbolic expressions. For a partial list, see Table 2.2.

```
> expand((1 + x)^2);
```

$$1 + 2x + x^2$$

```
> factor(%);
```

$$(1+x)^2$$

As mentioned in section 2.2, the ditto operator, %, is a shorthand notation for the previous result.

```
> Diff(sin(x), x);
```

$$\frac{d}{dx}\sin(x)$$

```
> value(%);
```

$$\cos(x)$$

```
> Sum(n^2, n);
```

$$\sum_{n} n^2$$

```
> value(%);
```

$$\frac{1}{3}\, n^3 - \frac{1}{2}\, n^2 + \frac{1}{6}\, n$$

Divide one polynomial in x by another.

```
> rem(x^3+x+1, x^2+x+1, x);
```

$$2 + x$$

Create a series.

```
> series(sin(x), x=0, 10);
```

$$x - \frac{1}{6}\, x^3 + \frac{1}{120}\, x^5 - \frac{1}{5040}\, x^7 + \frac{1}{362880}\, x^9 + \mathrm{O}(x^{10})$$

All the mathematical functions mentioned in the previous section also accept unknowns as arguments.

2.4 Assigning Expressions to Names

Using the ditto operator, or retyping a Maple expression every time you want to use it, is not always convenient, so Maple enables you to name an object. Use the following syntax for naming.

```
name := expression;
```

You can assign *any* Maple expression to a name.

```
> var := x;
```

$$var := x$$

```
> term := x*y;
```

$$term := x\, y$$

You can assign equations to names.

```
> eqn := x = y + 2;
```

$$eqn := x = y + 2$$

Maple names can include any alphanumeric characters and underscores, but they *cannot start with a number*. Also, avoid starting names with an underscore because Maple uses these names for internal classification. Valid Maple names include: `polynomial`, `test_data`, `RoOt_10cUs_pLoT`, and `value2`. Examples of *invalid* Maple names are `2ndphase` (because it begins with a number), and `x&y` (because `&` is not an alphanumeric character).

Define functions by using Maple's *arrow notation* (`->`). This notation allows you to evaluate a function when it appears in Maple expressions. At this point, you can do simple graphing of the function by using the `plot` command.

```
> f := x -> 2*x^2 -3*x +4;
```

$$f := x \to 2x^2 - 3x + 4$$

```
> plot (f(x), x= -5...5);
```

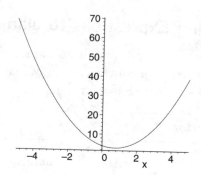

For more information on the `plot` command, see chapter 4 or enter `?plot` at the Maple prompt.

The assignment (`:=`) operator can then associate a function name with the function definition. The name of the function is on the left-hand side of the `:=`. The function definition (using the arrow notation) is on the right-hand side. The following statement defines `f` as the "squaring function."

```
> f := x -> x^2;
```

$$f := x \rightarrow x^2$$

Then, evaluating **f** at an argument produces the square of **f**'s argument.

> f(5);

$$25$$

> f(y+1);

$$(y+1)^2$$

Not all names are available for variables. Maple has some predefined and reserved names. If you try to assign to a name that is predefined or reserved, Maple displays a message, informing you that the name you have chosen is protected.

> Pi := 3.14;

Error, attempting to assign to 'Pi' which is protected

> set := {1, 2, 3};

Error, attempting to assign to 'set' which is protected

2.5 Basic Types of Maple Objects

This section examines basic types of Maple objects, including *expression sequences*, *lists*, *sets*, *arrays*, *tables*, and *strings*. These simple ideas are essential to the discussion in the rest of this book.

Expression Sequences

The basic Maple data structure is the *expression sequence*. This is simply a group of Maple expressions separated by commas.

> 1, 2, 3, 4;

$$1,\, 2,\, 3,\, 4$$

```
> x, y, z, w;
```

$$x,\, y,\, z,\, w$$

Expression sequences are neither lists nor sets. They are a distinct data structure within Maple and have their own properties. For example, they preserve the order and repetition of their elements. Items stay in the order in which you enter them. If you enter an element twice, both copies remain. Other properties of sequences will become apparent as you progress through this manual. Sequences are often used to build more sophisticated objects through such operations as concatenation.

Sequences extend the capabilities of many basic Maple operations. For example, concatenation is a basic name-forming operation. The concatenation operator in Maple is "||". You can use it in the following manner.

```
> a||b;
```

$$ab$$

When applying concatenation to a sequence, the operation affects each element. For example, if S is a sequence, then you can prepend the name a to each element in S by concatenating a and S.

```
> S := 1, 2, 3, 4;
```

$$S := 1,\, 2,\, 3,\, 4$$

```
> a||S;
```

$$a1,\, a2,\, a3,\, a4$$

You can also perform multiple assignments using expression sequences. For example

```
> f,g,h := 3, 6, 1;
```

$$f,\, g,\, h := 3,\, 6,\, 1$$

```
> f;
```

$$3$$

```
> h;
```

$$1$$

Lists

You create a *list* by enclosing any number of Maple objects (separated by commas) in square brackets.

```
> data_list := [1, 2, 3, 4, 5];
```

$$data\_list := [1,\, 2,\, 3,\, 4,\, 5]$$

```
> polynomials := [x^2+3, x^2+3*x-1, 2*x];
```

$$polynomials := [x^2 + 3,\, x^2 + 3\,x - 1,\, 2\,x]$$

```
> participants := [Kathy, Frank, Rene, Niklaus, Liz];
```

$$participants := [Kathy,\, Frank,\, Rene,\, Niklaus,\, Liz]$$

Thus, a list is an expression sequence enclosed in square brackets.

Maple preserves the order and repetition of elements in a list. Thus, [a,b,c], [b,c,a], and [a,a,b,c,a] are all different.

```
> [a,b,c], [b,c,a], [a,a,b,c,a];
```

$$[a,\, b,\, c],\ [b,\, c,\, a],\ [a,\, a,\, b,\, c,\, a]$$

The fact that order is preserved allows you to extract a particular element from a list without searching for it.

```
> letters := [a,b,c];
```

$$letters := [a,\, b,\, c]$$

```
> letters[2];
```

$$b$$

Use the **nops** command to determine the number of elements in a list.

```
> nops(letters);
```

$$3$$

Section 2.6 discusses this command, including its other uses, in more detail.

Sets

Maple supports *sets* in the mathematical sense. Commas separate the objects, as they do in a sequence or list, but the enclosing curly braces identify the object as a set.

```
> data_set := {1, -1, 0, 10, 2};
```

$$data\_set := \{-1, 0, 1, 2, 10\}$$

```
> unknowns := {x, y, z};
```

$$unknowns := \{x, y, z\}$$

Thus, a set is an expression sequence enclosed in curly braces.

Maple does not preserve order or repetition in a set. That is, Maple sets have the same properties as sets do in mathematics. Thus, the following three sets are identical.

```
> {a,b,c}, {c,b,a}, {a,a,b,c,a};
```

$$\{a, b, c\}, \{a, b, c\}, \{a, b, c\}$$

Remember that to Maple the integer 2 is distinct from the floating-point approximation 2.0. Thus, the following set has three elements, not two.

```
> {1, 2, 2.0};
```

$$\{1, 2, 2.0\}$$

The properties of sets make them a particularly useful concept in Maple, just as they are in mathematics. Maple provides many operations on sets, including the basic operations of *intersection* and *union* using the notation `intersect` and `union`.

```
> {a,b,c} union {c,d,e};
```

$$\{a,\ b,\ c,\ d,\ e\}$$

```
> {1,2,3,a,b,c} intersect {0,1,y,a};
```

$$\{1,\ a\}$$

The `nops` command counts the number of elements in a set or list.

```
> nops(%);
```

$$2$$

For more details on the `nops` command, see section 2.6.

A common and very useful command, often used on sets, is `map`. Mapping applies a function simultaneously to all the elements of any structure.

```
> numbers := {0, Pi/3, Pi/2, Pi};
```

$$numbers := \{0,\ \pi,\ \frac{1}{3}\pi,\ \frac{1}{2}\pi\}$$

```
> map(g, numbers);
```

$$\{g(0),\ g(\pi),\ g(\frac{1}{3}\pi),\ g(\frac{1}{2}\pi)\}$$

```
> map(sin, numbers);
```

$$\{0,\ 1,\ \frac{1}{2}\sqrt{3}\}$$

Further examples demonstrating the use of `map` appear in sections 2.6 and 5.3.

Operations on Sets and Lists

The `member` command verifies membership in sets and lists.

```
> participants := [Kate, Tom, Steve];
```

$$participants := [Kate,\ Tom,\ Steve]$$

```
> member(Tom, participants);
```

$$true$$

```
> data_set := {5, 6, 3, 7};
```

$$data\_set := \{3,\ 5,\ 6,\ 7\}$$

```
> member(2, data_set);
```

$$false$$

To choose items from lists, use the subscript notation, `[n]`, where n identifies the position of the desired element in the list.

```
> participants[2];
```

$$Tom$$

Maple recognizes *empty* sets and lists, that is, lists or sets that have no elements.

```
> empty_set := {};
```

$$empty\_set := \{\}$$

```
> empty_list := [];
```

$$empty\_list := []$$

You can create a new set from other sets by using, for example, the `union` command. Delete items from sets by using the `minus` command.

```
> old_set := {2, 3, 4} union {};
```

$$old\_set := \{2, 3, 4\}$$

```
> new_set := old_set union {2, 5};
```

$$new\_set := \{2, 3, 4, 5\}$$

```
> third_set := old_set minus {2, 5};
```

$$third\_set := \{3, 4\}$$

Arrays

Arrays are an extension of the concept of the list data structure. Think of a list as a group of items in which you associate each item with a positive integer, its index, that represents its position in the list. The Maple **array** data structure is a generalization of this idea. Each element is still associated with an index, but an array is not restricted to one dimension. In addition, indices can also be zero or negative. Furthermore, you can define or change the array's individual elements without redefining it entirely.

Declare the array so Maple knows the dimensions you want to use.

```
> squares := array(1..3);
```

$$squares := \mathrm{array}(1..3, [])$$

Assign the array elements. Multiple commands can be entered at one command prompt provided each ends with a colon or semicolon.

```
> squares[1] := 1;  squares[2] := 2^2;  squares[3] := 3^2;
```

$$squares_1 := 1$$

$$squares_2 := 4$$

$$squares_3 := 9$$

Or, if you prefer, do both simultaneously.

```
> cubes := array( 1..3, [1,8,27] );
```

$$cubes := [1, 8, 27]$$

You can select a single element using the same notation applied to lists.

```
> squares[2];
```

$$4$$

You must declare arrays in advance. To see the array's contents, you must use a command such as `print`.

```
> squares;
```

$$squares$$

```
> print(squares);
```

$$[1, 4, 9]$$

The preceding array has only one dimension, but arrays can have more than one dimension. Define a 3×3 array.

```
> pwrs := array(1..3,1..3);
```

$$pwrs := \mathrm{array}(1..3, 1..3, [])$$

This array has dimension two (two sets of indices). To begin, assign the array elements of the first row.

```
> pwrs[1,1] := 1;  pwrs[1,2] := 1;  pwrs[1,3] := 1;
```

$$pwrs_{1,1} := 1$$

$$pwrs_{1,2} := 1$$

$$pwrs_{1,3} := 1$$

Now continue for the rest of the array. If you prefer, you can end each command with a colon (:), instead of the usual semicolon (;), to suppress the output. Both the colon and semicolon are statement separators.

```
> pwrs[2,1] := 2:  pwrs[2,2] := 4:  pwrs[2,3] := 8:
> pwrs[3,1] := 3:  pwrs[3,2] := 9:  pwrs[3,3] := 27:
> print(pwrs);
```

$$\begin{bmatrix} 1 & 1 & 1 \\ 2 & 4 & 8 \\ 3 & 9 & 27 \end{bmatrix}$$

You can select an element by specifying both the row and column.

> `pwrs[2,3];`

$$8$$

You can define a two-dimensional array and its elements simultaneously by using a similar method employed for the one-dimensional example shown earlier. To do so, use lists within lists. That is, make a list where each element is a list that contains the elements of one row of the array. Thus, you could define the `pwrs` array as follows.

> `pwrs2 := array( 1..3, 1..3, [[1,1,1], [2,4,8], [3,9,27]] );`

$$pwrs2 := \begin{bmatrix} 1 & 1 & 1 \\ 2 & 4 & 8 \\ 3 & 9 & 27 \end{bmatrix}$$

Arrays are by no means limited to two dimensions, but those of higher order are more difficult to display. You can declare all the elements of the array as you define its dimension.

> `array3 := array( 1..2, 1..2, 1..2,`
> `[[[1,2],[3,4]], [[5,6],[7,8]]] );`

$$array3 := \mathrm{array}(1..2,\ 1..2,\ 1..2, [$$
$$(1, 1, 1) = 1$$
$$(1, 1, 2) = 2$$
$$(1, 2, 1) = 3$$
$$(1, 2, 2) = 4$$
$$(2, 1, 1) = 5$$
$$(2, 1, 2) = 6$$
$$(2, 2, 1) = 7$$
$$(2, 2, 2) = 8$$
$$])$$

Maple does not automatically expand the name of an array to the representation of all the elements. Thus, in some commands, you must specify explicitly that you want to perform an operation on the elements.

Suppose that you want to replace each occurrence of the number 2 in **pwrs** with the number 9. To do substitutions such as this, you can use the **subs** command. The basic syntax is

```
subs( x=expr1, y=expr2, ... , main_expr )
```

For example, to substitute $x + y$ for z in an equation, do the following.

```
> expr := z^2 + 3;
```

$$expr := z^2 + 3$$

```
> subs( {z=x+y}, expr);
```

$$(x + y)^2 + 3$$

You might, however, be disappointed when the following call to **subs** does not work.

```
> subs( {2=9}, pwrs );
```

$$pwrs$$

You must instead force Maple to fully evaluate the name of the array to the component level and not just to its name, using the command **evalm**.

```
> subs( {2=9}, evalm(pwrs) );
```

$$\begin{bmatrix} 1 & 1 & 1 \\ 9 & 4 & 8 \\ 3 & 9 & 27 \end{bmatrix}$$

Not only does this cause the substitution to occur in the components as expected, but full evaluation also displays the array's elements, just as when you use the **print** command.

```
> evalm(pwrs);
```

$$\begin{bmatrix} 1 & 1 & 1 \\ 2 & 4 & 8 \\ 3 & 9 & 27 \end{bmatrix}$$

Tables

A *table* is an extension of the concept of the array data structure. The difference between an array and a table is that a table can have *anything* for indices, not just integers.

```
> translate := table([one=un,two=deux,three=trois]);
```

$$translate := \text{table}([three = trois, \ one = un, \ two = deux])$$

```
> translate[two];
```

$$deux$$

Although at first they may seem to have little advantage over arrays, table structures are very powerful. Tables enable you to work with natural notation for data structures. For example, you can display the physical properties of materials using a Maple table.

```
> earth_data := table( [ mass=[5.976*10^24,kg],
>                        radius=[6.378164*10^6,m],
>                        circumference=[4.00752*10^7,m] ] );
```

$$earth\_data := \text{table}([mass = [0.5976000000\,10^{25}, \ kg],$$
$$radius = [0.6378164000\,10^{7}, \ m],$$
$$circumference = [0.4007520000\,10^{8}, \ m]$$
$$])$$

```
> earth_data[mass];
```

$$[0.5976000000\,10^{25}, \ kg]$$

In this example, each index is a name and each entry is a list. In fact, this is a rather simple case. Often, much more general indices are useful.

For example, you could construct a table which has algebraic formulæ for indices and the derivatives of these formulæ as values.

Strings

A *string* is also an object in Maple and is created by enclosing any number of characters in double quotes.

```
> "This is a string.";
```

$$\text{``This is a string.''}$$

They are nearly indivisible constructs that stand only for themselves; they cannot be assigned a value.

```
> "my age" := 32;
```

```
Error, invalid left hand side of assignment
```

Like elements of lists or arrays, the individual characters of a string can be indexed with square bracket notation.

```
> mystr := "I ate the whole thing.";
```

$$mystr := \text{``I ate the whole thing.''}$$

```
> mystr[3..5];
```

$$\text{``ate''}$$

```
> mystr[11..-2];
```

$$\text{``whole thing''}$$

A negative index represents a character position counted from the right end of the string. In the example above, -2 represents the second last character.

The concatenation operator, "||", or the **cat** command is used to join two strings together, and the **length** command is used to determine the number of characters in a string.

```
> newstr := cat("I can't believe ", mystr);
```

$$newstr := \text{``I can't believe I ate the whole thing.''}$$

```
> length(newstr);
```

$$38$$

There are other commands that operate on strings and many more that take strings as input. For examples, refer to **?StringTools**.

2.6 Expression Manipulation

Many of Maple's commands concentrate on manipulating expressions. This includes manipulating results of Maple commands into a familiar form, or a form with which you want to work. This can also involve manipulating your own expressions into a form with which Maple can work. This section introduces the most commonly used commands in this area.

The simplify Command

You can use this command to apply simplification rules to an expression. Maple has simplification rules for various types of expressions and forms, including trigonometric functions, radicals, logarithmic functions, exponential functions, powers, and various special functions.

```
> expr := cos(x)^5 + sin(x)^4 + 2*cos(x)^2
> - 2*sin(x)^2 - cos(2*x);
```

$$expr :=$$
$$\cos(x)^5 + \sin(x)^4 + 2\cos(x)^2 - 2\sin(x)^2 - \cos(2\,x)$$

```
> simplify(expr);
```

$$\cos(x)^4\,(\cos(x) + 1)$$

To perform only a certain type of simplification, specify the type you want.

```
> simplify(sin(x)^2 + ln(2*y) + cos(x)^2);
```

$$1 + \ln(2) + \ln(y)$$

```
> simplify(sin(x)^2 + ln(2*y) + cos(x)^2, 'trig');
```

$$1 + \ln(2\,y)$$

```
> simplify(sin(x)^2 + ln(2*y) + cos(x)^2, 'ln');
```

$$\sin(x)^2 + \ln(2) + \ln(y) + \cos(x)^2$$

With the *side relations* feature, you can apply your own simplification rules.

```
> siderel := {sin(x)^2 + cos(x)^2 = 1};
```

$$siderel := \{\sin(x)^2 + \cos(x)^2 = 1\}$$

```
> trig_expr := sin(x)^3 - sin(x)*cos(x)^2 + 3*cos(x)^3;
```

$$trig\_expr := \sin(x)^3 - \sin(x)\cos(x)^2 + 3\cos(x)^3$$

```
> simplify(trig_expr, siderel);
```

$$2\sin(x)^3 - 3\cos(x)\sin(x)^2 + 3\cos(x) - \sin(x)$$

The factor Command

This command factors polynomial expressions.

```
> big_poly := x^5 - x^4 - 7*x^3 + x^2 + 6*x;
```

$$big\_poly := x^5 - x^4 - 7\,x^3 + x^2 + 6\,x$$

```
> factor(big_poly);
```

$$x\,(x-1)\,(x-3)\,(x+2)\,(x+1)$$

```
> rat_expr := (x^3 - y^3)/(x^4 - y^4);
```

$$rat\_expr := \frac{x^3 - y^3}{x^4 - y^4}$$

Both the numerator and denominator contain the common factor $x-y$. Thus, factoring cancels these terms.

```
> factor(rat_expr);
```

$$\frac{x^2 + x\,y + y^2}{(y + x)\,(x^2 + y^2)}$$

Maple can factor both univariate and multivariate polynomials over the domain the coefficients specify. You can also factor polynomials over algebraic extensions. For details, refer to **?factor**.

The expand **Command**

The **expand** command is essentially the reverse of **factor**. It causes the expansion of multiplied terms as well as a number of other expansions. This is among the most useful of the manipulation commands. Although you might imagine that with a name like **expand** the result would be larger and more complex than the original expression; this is not always the case. In fact, expanding some expressions results in substantial simplification.

```
> expand((x+1)*(x+2));
```

$$x^2 + 3\,x + 2$$

```
> expand(sin(x+y));
```

$$\sin(y)\cos(x) + \cos(y)\sin(x)$$

```
> expand(exp(a+ln(b)));
```

$$e^a\,b$$

The **expand** command is quite flexible. Not only can you specify that certain subexpressions be unchanged by the expansion, but you can also program custom expansion rules.

Although the **simplify** command may seem to be the most useful command, this is misleading. Unfortunately, the word *simplify* is rather vague. When you request to **simplify** an expression, Maple examines your expression, tests out many techniques, and then tries applying the appropriate simplification rules. However, this might take a little time. As well, Maple may not be able to determine what you want to accomplish since universal mathematical rules do not define what is simpler.

When you do know which manipulations will make your expression simpler for you, specify them directly. In particular, the **expand** command is among the most useful. It frequently results in substantial simplification, and also leaves expressions in a convenient form for many other commands.

The convert Command

This command converts expressions between different forms. For a list of common conversions, see Table 2.3.

```
> convert(cos(x),exp);
```

$$\frac{1}{2} e^{(x\,I)} + \frac{1}{2}\frac{1}{e^{(x\,I)}}$$

```
> convert(1/2*exp(x) + 1/2*exp(-x),trig);
```

$$\cosh(x)$$

```
> A := Matrix([[a,b],[c,d]]);
```

$$A := \begin{bmatrix} a & b \\ c & d \end{bmatrix}$$

```
> convert(A, 'listlist');
```

$$[[a,\,b],\,[c,\,d]]$$

```
> convert(A, 'set');
```

$$\{a,\,b,\,d,\,c\}$$

```
> convert(%, 'list');
```

$$[a,\,b,\,d,\,c]$$

Table 2.3 Common Conversions

Argument	Description
polynom	series to polynomials
exp, expln, expsincos	trigonometric expressions to exponential form
parfrac	rational expressions to partial fraction form
rational	floating-point numbers to rational form
radians, degrees	between degrees and radians
set, list, listlist	between data structures
temperature	between temperature scales
units	between units

The normal Command

This command transforms rational expressions into *factored normal form*,

$$\frac{numerator}{denominator},$$

where the *numerator* and *denominator* are relatively prime polynomials with integer coefficients.

```
> rat_expr_2 := (x^2 - y^2)/(x - y)^3 ;
```

$$rat\_expr\_2 := \frac{x^2 - y^2}{(-y + x)^3}$$

```
> normal(rat_expr_2);
```

$$\frac{y + x}{(-y + x)^2}$$

```
> normal(rat_expr_2, 'expanded');
```

$$\frac{y + x}{y^2 - 2xy + x^2}$$

The **expanded** option transforms rational expressions into *expanded normal form*.

The combine Command

This command combines terms in sums, products, and powers into a single term. These transformations are, in some cases, the reverse of the transformations that **expand** applies.

```
> combine(exp(x)^2*exp(y),exp);
```

$$e^{(2x+y)}$$

```
> combine((x^a)^2, power);
```

$$x^{(2a)}$$

The map Command

This command is most useful when working with lists, sets, or arrays. It provides an especially convenient means for working with multiple solutions or for applying an operation to each element of an array.

The **map** command applies a command to each element of a data structure or expression. While it is possible to write program structures such as loops to accomplish these tasks, you should not underestimate the convenience and power of the **map** command. The **map** command is one of the most useful commands in Maple.

```
> map( f, [a,b,c] );
```

$$[f(a), f(b), f(c)]$$

```
> data_list := [0, Pi/2, 3*Pi/2, 2*Pi];
```

$$data\_list := [0, \frac{1}{2}\pi, \frac{3}{2}\pi, 2\pi]$$

```
> map(sin, data_list);
```

$$[0, 1, -1, 0]$$

If you give the **map** command more than two arguments, Maple passes the last argument(s) to the initial command.

```
> map( f, [a,b,c], x, y );
```

$$[f(a, x, y), f(b, x, y), f(c, x, y)]$$

For example, to differentiate each item in a list with respect to x, you can use the following commands.

```
> fcn_list := [sin(x),ln(x),x^2];
```

$$fcn\_list := [\sin(x), \ln(x), x^2]$$

```
> map(Diff, fcn_list, x);
```

$$[\frac{d}{dx}\sin(x), \frac{d}{dx}\ln(x), \frac{d}{dx}(x^2)]$$

```
> map(value, %);
```

$$[\cos(x), \frac{1}{x}, 2\,x]$$

Not only can the procedure be an existing command, but you can also create an operation to map onto a list. For example, suppose that you want to square each element of a list. Replace each element (represented by x) with its square (x^2).

```
> map(x->x^2, [-1,0,1,2,3]);
```

$$[1, 0, 1, 4, 9]$$

The lhs and rhs Commands

These two commands take the left-hand side and right-hand side of an expression, respectively.

```
> eqn1 := x+y=z+3;
```

$$eqn1 := y + x = z + 3$$

```
> lhs(eqn1);
```

$$y + x$$

```
> rhs(eqn1);
```

$$z + 3$$

The numer and denom Commands

These two commands take the numerator and denominator of a rational expression, respectively.

```
> numer(3/4);
```

$$3$$

```
> denom(1/(1 + x));
```

$$x + 1$$

The nops and op Commands

These two commands are useful for breaking expressions into parts and extracting subexpressions.

The nops command returns the number of parts in an expression.

```
> nops(x^2);
```

$$2$$

```
> nops(x + y + z);
```

$$3$$

The op command allows you to access the parts of an expression. It returns the parts as a sequence.

```
> op(x^2);
```

$$x, 2$$

You can also specify items by number or range.

```
> op(1, x^2);
```

$$x$$

```
> op(2, x^2);
```

$$2$$

```
> op(2..-2, x+y+z+w);
```

$$y, z$$

Common Questions about Expression Manipulation

How do I Substitute for a Product of Two Unknowns

Use side relations to specify an identity. Substituting directly does not usually work, since Maple searches for an exact match before substituting.

```
> expr := a^3*b^2;
```

$$expr := a^3 b^2$$

```
> subs(a*b=5, expr);
```

$$a^3 b^2$$

The `subs` command was unsuccessful in its attempt to substitute. Try the `simplify` command this time to get the desired answer.

```
> simplify(expr, {a*b=5});
```

$$25\,a$$

You can also try the `algsubs` command, which performs an algebraic substitution.

```
> algsubs(a*b=5, expr);
```

$$25\,a$$

Why is the Result of `simplify` Not the Simplest Form

For example:

```
> expr2 := cos(x)*(sec(x)-cos(x));
```

$$expr2 := \cos(x)\,(\sec(x) - \cos(x))$$

```
> simplify(expr2);
```

$$1 - \cos(x)^2$$

The expected form was $\sin(x)^2$.

Again, use side relations to specify the identity.

```
> simplify(%, {1-cos(x)^2=sin(x)^2});
```

$$\sin(x)^2$$

The issue of simplification is a complicated one because it is difficult to define the *simplest* form of an expression. One user's idea of a simple form may be vastly different from another user's; indeed, the idea of the simplest form can vary from situation to situation.

How do I Factor out the Constant from $2x + 2y$ Currently, this operation is not possible in Maple because its simplifier automatically distributes the number over the product, believing that a sum is simpler than a product. In most cases, this is true.

If you enter the expression

```
> 2*(x + y);
```

$$2x + 2y$$

you see that Maple automatically multiplies the constant into the expression.

How can you then deal with such expressions, when you need to factor out constants, or negative signs? Should you need to factor such expressions, try this "clever" substitution.

```
> expr3 := 2*(x + y);
```

$$expr3 := 2x + 2y$$

```
> subs( 2=two, expr3 );
```

$$x\,two + y\,two$$

```
> factor(%);
```

$$two\,(x + y)$$

2.7   Conclusion

In this chapter you have seen many of the types of objects which Maple is capable of manipulating, including sequences, sets, and lists. You have seen a number of commands, including `expand`, `factor`, and `simplify`, that are useful for manipulating and simplifying algebraic expressions. Others, such as `map`, are useful for sets, lists, and arrays. Meanwhile, `subs` is useful almost any time.

In the next chapter, you will learn to apply these concepts to solve systems of equations, one of the most fundamental problems in mathematics. As you learn about new commands, observe how the concepts of this chapter are used in setting up problems and manipulating solutions.

3 Finding Solutions

This chapter introduces the key concepts needed for quick, concise problem solving in Maple. By learning how to use such tools as `solve`, `map`, `subs`, and `unapply`, you can save yourself a substantial amount of work. In addition, this chapter examines how these commands interoperate.

3.1 Simple `solve`

Maple's `solve` command is a general-purpose equation solver. It takes a set of one or more equations and attempts to solve them exactly for the specified set of unknowns. (Recall from section 2.5 that you use braces to denote a set.) In the following examples, you are solving one equation for one unknown, so each set contains only one element.

```
> solve({x^2=4}, {x});
```

$$\{x = 2\}, \{x = -2\}$$

```
> solve({a*x^2+b*x+c=0}, {x});
```

$$\{x = \frac{1}{2} \frac{-b + \sqrt{b^2 - 4\,a\,c}}{a}\}, \{x = \frac{1}{2} \frac{-b - \sqrt{b^2 - 4\,a\,c}}{a}\}$$

Maple returns each possible solution as a set. Since both of these equations have two solutions, Maple returns a sequence of solution sets. If you do not specify any unknowns in the equation, Maple solves for all of them.

```
> solve({x+y=0});
```

$$\{x = -y, \, y = y\}$$

Here you get only one solution set containing two equations. This result means that y can take any value, while x is the negative of y. This solution is parameterized with respect to y.

If you give an expression rather than an equation, Maple automatically assumes that the expression is equal to zero.

```
> solve({x^3-13*x+12}, {x});
```

$$\{x = 1\}, \, \{x = 3\}, \, \{x = -4\}$$

The **solve** command can also handle systems of equations.

```
> solve({x+2*y=3, y+1/x=1}, {x,y});
```

$$\{x = -1, \, y = 2\}, \, \{x = 2, \, y = \frac{1}{2}\}$$

Although you do not always need the braces (denoting a set) around either the equation or variable, using them forces Maple to return the solution as a set, which is usually the most convenient form. For example, it is a common practice to check your solutions by substituting them into the original equations. The following example demonstrates this procedure.

As a set of equations, the solution is in an ideal form for the **subs** command. You might first give the set of equations a name, like **eqns**, for instance.

```
> eqns := {x+2*y=3, y+1/x=1};
```

$$eqns := \{x + 2\,y = 3, \, y + \frac{1}{x} = 1\}$$

Then solve.

```
> soln := solve( eqns, {x,y} );
```

$$soln := \{x = -1, \, y = 2\}, \, \{x = 2, \, y = \frac{1}{2}\}$$

This produces two solutions:

```
> soln[1];
```

$${x = -1, y = 2}$$

and

```
> soln[2];
```

$${x = 2, y = \frac{1}{2}}$$

Verifying Solutions

To check the solutions, substitute them into the original set of equations by using the two-parameter `eval` command.

```
> eval( eqns, soln[1] );
```

$${1 = 1, 3 = 3}$$

```
> eval( eqns, soln[2] );
```

$${1 = 1, 3 = 3}$$

For verifying solutions, you will find that this method is generally the most convenient.

Observe that this application of the `eval` command has other uses. Suppose you wish to extract the value of x from the first solution. Again, the best tool is the `eval` command.

```
> x1 := eval( x, soln[1] );
```

$$x1 := -1$$

Alternatively, you could extract the first solution for y.

```
> y1 := eval(y, soln[1]);
```

$$y1 := 2$$

You can use this evaluation trick to convert solution sets to other forms. For example, you can construct a `list` from the first solution where x is the first element and y is the second. First construct a `list` with the *variables* in the same order as you want the corresponding *solutions*.

```
> [x,y];
```

$$[x, y]$$

Then simply evaluate this list at the first solution.

```
> eval([x,y], soln[1]);
```

$$[-1, 2]$$

The first solution is now a list.

Instead, if you prefer that the solution for y comes first, evaluate [y,x] at the solution.

```
> eval([y,x], soln[1]);
```

$$[2, -1]$$

Since Maple typically returns solutions in the form of sets (in which the order of objects is uncertain), remembering this method for extracting solutions is useful.

The map command is another useful command that allows you to apply one operation to all solutions. For example, try substituting *both* solutions.

The map command applies the operation specified as its first argument to its second argument.

```
> map(f, [a,b,c], y, z);
```

$$[\mathrm{f}(a,\, y,\, z),\, \mathrm{f}(b,\, y,\, z),\, \mathrm{f}(c,\, y,\, z)]$$

Due to the syntactical design of map, it cannot perform multiple function applications to sequences. Consider the previous solution sequence, for example,

```
> soln;
```

$$\{x = -1,\, y = 2\},\, \{x = 2,\, y = \frac{1}{2}\}$$

Enclose soln in square brackets to convert it to a list.

```
> [soln];
```

$$[\{x = -1, \, y = 2\}, \, \{x = 2, \, y = \frac{1}{2}\}]$$

Now use the following command to substitute *each* of the solutions simultaneously into the original equations, **eqns**.

```
> map(subs, [soln], eqns);
```

$$[\{1 = 1, \, 3 = 3\}, \, \{1 = 1, \, 3 = 3\}]$$

This method can be valuable if your equation has many solutions, or if you are unsure of the number of solutions that a certain command will produce.

Restricting Solutions

You can limit solutions by specifying inequalities with the **solve** command.

```
> solve({x^2=y^2},{x,y});
```

$$\{x = -y, \, y = y\}, \, \{x = y, \, y = y\}$$

```
> solve({x^2=y^2, x<>y},{x,y});
```

$$\{x = -y, \, y = y\}$$

Consider this system of five equations in five unknowns.

```
> eqn1 := x+2*y+3*z+4*t+5*u=41:
> eqn2 := 5*x+5*y+4*z+3*t+2*u=20:
> eqn3 := 3*y+4*z-8*t+2*u=125:
> eqn4 := x+y+z+t+u=9:
> eqn5 := 8*x+4*z+3*t+2*u=11:
```

Now solve the system for all variables.

```
> s1 := solve({eqn1,eqn2,eqn3,eqn4,eqn5}, {x,y,z,t,u});
```

$$s1 := \{x = 2, \, t = -11, \, z = -1, \, y = 3, \, u = 16\}$$

You can also choose to solve for a subset of the unknowns. Then Maple returns the solutions in terms of the other unknowns.

```
> s2 := solve({eqn1,eqn2,eqn3}, { x, y, z});
```

$$s2 := \{x = -\frac{527}{13} - 7t - \frac{28}{13}u, \; z = -\frac{70}{13} - 7t - \frac{59}{13}u,$$
$$y = \frac{635}{13} + 12t + \frac{70}{13}u\}$$

Exploring Solutions

You can explore the parametric solutions found at the end of the previous section. For example, evaluate the solution at $u = 1$ and $t = 1$.

```
> eval( s2, {u=1,t=1} );
```

$$\{x = \frac{-646}{13}, \; z = \frac{-220}{13}, \; y = \frac{861}{13}\}$$

Suppose that you require the solutions from **solve** in a particular order. Since you cannot fix the order of elements in a set, **solve** will not necessarily return your solutions in the order x, y, z. However, lists do preserve order. Try the following.

```
> eval( [x,y,z], s2 );
```

$$[-\frac{527}{13} - 7t - \frac{28}{13}u, \; \frac{635}{13} + 12t + \frac{70}{13}u, \; -\frac{70}{13} - 7t - \frac{59}{13}u]$$

This command not only fixed the order, but it also extracted the right-hand side of the equations. Because the order is fixed, you know the solution for each variable. This capability is particularly useful if you want to plot the solution surface.

```
> plot3d(%, u=0..2, t=0..2, axes=BOXED);
```

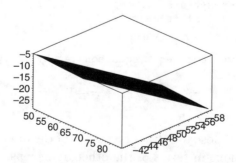

The unapply **Command**

For convenience, define $x = x(u,t)$, $y = y(u,t)$, and $z = z(u,t)$, that is, convert the solutions to functions. Recall that you can easily select a solution *expression* for a particular variable using `eval`.

```
> eval( x, s2 );
```

$$-\frac{527}{13} - 7t - \frac{28}{13}u$$

However, this is an *expression* for x and not a function.

```
> x(1,1);
```

$$x(1, 1)$$

To convert the expression to a function you need another important command, **unapply**. To use it, provide **unapply** with the expression *and* the independent variables. For example,

```
> f := unapply(x^2 + y^2 + 4, x, y);
```

$$f := (x, y) \to x^2 + y^2 + 4$$

produces the function, f, of x and y that maps (x,y) to $x^2 + y^2 + 4$. This new function is easy to use.

```
> f(a,b);
```

$$a^2 + b^2 + 4$$

Thus, to make your solution for x a function of both u and t, the first step is to obtain the *expression* for x, as above.

```
> eval(x, s2);
```

$$-\frac{527}{13} - 7t - \frac{28}{13}u$$

Then use **unapply** to turn it into a function of u and t.

```
> x := unapply(%, u, t);
```

$$x := (u,\, t) \rightarrow -\frac{527}{13} - 7\,t - \frac{28}{13}\,u$$

> x(1,1);

$$\frac{-646}{13}$$

You can create the functions y and z in the same manner.

> eval(y,s2);

$$\frac{635}{13} + 12\,t + \frac{70}{13}\,u$$

> y := unapply(%,u,t);

$$y := (u,\, t) \rightarrow \frac{635}{13} + 12\,t + \frac{70}{13}\,u$$

> eval(z,s2);

$$-\frac{70}{13} - 7\,t - \frac{59}{13}\,u$$

> z := unapply(%, u, t);

$$z := (u,\, t) \rightarrow -\frac{70}{13} - 7\,t - \frac{59}{13}\,u$$

> y(1,1), z(1,1);

$$\frac{861}{13},\ \frac{-220}{13}$$

The assign Command

The **assign** command also allocates values to unknowns. For example, instead of defining x, y, and z as functions, assign each to the expression on the right-hand side of the corresponding equation.

```
> assign( s2 );
> x, y, z;
```

$$-\frac{527}{13} - 7\,t - \frac{28}{13}\,u, \ \frac{635}{13} + 12\,t + \frac{70}{13}\,u, \ -\frac{70}{13} - 7\,t - \frac{59}{13}\,u$$

Think of the **assign** command as turning the "=" signs in the solution set into ":=" signs.

The **assign** command is convenient if you want to assign expressions to names. *Remember, though, that while this command is useful for quickly assigning solutions, it cannot create functions.*

This next example incorporates solving differential equations, which section 3.6 discusses in further detail. To begin, assign the solution.

```
> s3 := dsolve( {diff(f(x),x)=6*x^2+1, f(0)=0}, {f(x)} );
```

$$s3 := \mathrm{f}(x) = 2\,x^3 + x$$

```
> assign( s3 );
```

However, you have yet to create a function.

```
> f(x);
```

$$2\,x^3 + x$$

produces the expected answer, but despite appearances, f(x) is simply a name for the *expression* $2x^3 + x$ and *not* a *function*. Call the function f using an argument other than x.

```
> f(1);
```

$$\mathrm{f}(1)$$

The reason for this apparently odd behavior is that **assign** asks Maple to do the assignment

```
> f(x) := 2*x^3 + x;
```

$$\mathrm{f}(x) := 2\,x^3 + x$$

which is not at all the same as the assignment

```
> f := x -> 2*x^3 + x;
```

$$f := x \to 2\,x^3 + x$$

The former defines the value of the function f for only the special argument x. The latter defines the function $f\colon x \mapsto 2x^3 + x$ so that it works whether you say $f(x)$, $f(y)$, or $f(1)$.

To define the solution f as a function of x use **unapply**.

```
> eval(f(x),s3);
```

$$2\,x^3 + x$$

```
> f := unapply(%, x);
```

$$f := x \to 2\,x^3 + x$$

```
> f(1);
```

$$3$$

The RootOf Command

Maple occasionally returns solutions in terms of the RootOf command. The following example demonstrates this point.

```
> solve({x^5 - 2*x + 3 = 0},{x});
```

$$\{x = \mathrm{RootOf}(\_Z^5 - 2\,\_Z + 3,\ index = 1)\},$$
$$\{x = \mathrm{RootOf}(\_Z^5 - 2\,\_Z + 3,\ index = 2)\},$$
$$\{x = \mathrm{RootOf}(\_Z^5 - 2\,\_Z + 3,\ index = 3)\},$$
$$\{x = \mathrm{RootOf}(\_Z^5 - 2\,\_Z + 3,\ index = 4)\},$$
$$\{x = \mathrm{RootOf}(\_Z^5 - 2\,\_Z + 3,\ index = 5)\}$$

RootOf(expr) is a placeholder for all the roots of expr. This indicates that x is a root of the polynomial $z^5 - 2z + 3$, while the index parameter numbers and orders the solutions. This can be useful if your algebra is over a field different from the complex numbers. By using the **evalf** command, you obtain an explicit form of the complex roots.

```
> evalf(%);
```

$$\{x = 0.9585321812 + 0.4984277790 \, I\},$$
$$\{x = -0.2467292569 + 1.320816347 \, I\},$$
$$\{x = -1.423605849\},$$
$$\{x = -0.2467292569 - 1.320816347 \, I\},$$
$$\{x = 0.9585321812 - 0.4984277790 \, I\}$$

A general expression for the roots of degree five polynomials in terms of radicals does not exist.

3.2   Solving Numerically: `fsolve`

The `fsolve` command is the numeric equivalent of `solve`. The `fsolve` command finds the roots of the equation(s) by using a variation of Newton's method, producing approximate (floating-point) solutions.

```
> fsolve({cos(x)-x = 0}, {x});
```

$$\{x = 0.7390851332\}$$

For a general equation, `fsolve` searches for a single real root. For a polynomial, however, it looks for all *real* roots.

```
> poly :=3*x^4 - 16*x^3 - 3*x^2 + 13*x + 16;
```

$$poly := 3\,x^4 - 16\,x^3 - 3\,x^2 + 13\,x + 16$$

```
> fsolve({poly},{x});
```

$$\{x = 1.324717957\}, \{x = 5.333333333\}$$

To look for more than one root of a general equation, use the `avoid` option.

```
> fsolve({sin(x)=0}, {x});
```

$$\{x = 0.\}$$

```
> fsolve({sin(x)=0}, {x}, avoid={x=0});
```

$$\{x = -3.141592654\}$$

To find a specified number of roots in a polynomial, use the `maxsols` option.

```
> fsolve({poly}, {x}, maxsols=1);
```

$$\{x = 1.324717957\}$$

By using the `complex` option, Maple searches for complex roots in addition to real roots.

```
> fsolve({poly}, {x}, complex);
```

$$\{x = -0.6623589786 - 0.5622795121\, I\},$$
$$\{x = -0.6623589786 + 0.5622795121\, I\},$$
$$\{x = 1.324717957\}, \{x = 5.333333333\}$$

You can also specify a range in which to look for a root.

```
> fsolve({cos(x)=0}, {x}, Pi..2*Pi);
```

$$\{x = 4.712388980\}$$

In some cases, `fsolve` may fail to find a root even if one exists. In these cases, specifying a range should help. To increase the accuracy of the solutions, you can increase the value of the special variable, `Digits`. Note that in the following example the solution is not guaranteed to be accurate to thirty digits, but rather, Maple performs all steps in the solution to at least thirty significant digits rather than the default of ten.

```
> Digits := 30;
```

$$Digits := 30$$

```
> fsolve({cos(x)=0}, {x});
```

$$\{x = 1.57079632679489661923132169164\}$$

Limitations on `solve`

The `solve` command cannot solve all problems. Remember that Maple's approach is algorithmic, and it does not necessarily have the ability to use the shortcuts that you might use when solving the problem by hand.

Mathematically, polynomials of degree five or higher do not have a solution in terms of radicals. Maple attempts to solve them, but you may have to resort to a numerical solution.

Solving trigonometric equations can also be difficult. In fact, working with all transcendental equations is quite difficult.

```
> solve({sin(x)=0}, {x});
```

$$\{x = 0\}$$

Note that Maple returns only one of an infinite number of solutions. However, if you set the environment variable _EnvAllSolutions to true, Maple returns the entire set of solutions.

```
> _EnvAllSolutions := true;
```

$$\_EnvAllSolutions := true$$

```
> solve({sin(x)=0}, {x});
```

$$\{x = \pi\_Z1^{\sim}\}$$

The prefix _Z on the variable indicates that it has integer values. The tilde (~) indicates that there is an assumption on the variable, namely that it is an integer. In addition, with the `fsolve` command you can specify the range in which to look for a solution. Thereby you may gain more control over the solution.

```
> fsolve({sin(x)=0}, {x}, 3..4);
```

$$\{x = 3.141592653589793238462643383328\}$$

These types of problems are common to all symbolic computation systems, and are symptoms of the natural limitations of an algorithmic approach to equation solving.

When using `solve`, remember to check your results. The next example highlights an issue that can arise as a result of Maple's treatment of removable singularities.

```
> expr := (x-1)^2/(x^2-1);
```

$$expr := \frac{(x-1)^2}{x^2-1}$$

Maple finds a solution

```
> soln := solve({expr=0},{x});
```

$$soln := \{x = 1\}$$

but when you evaluate the expression at 1, you get 0/0.

```
> eval(expr, soln);
```

```
Error, numeric exception: division by zero
```

The limit shows that $x = 1$ is nearly a solution.

```
> Limit(expr, x=1);
```

$$\lim_{x \to 1} \frac{(x-1)^2}{x^2-1}$$

```
> value (%);
```

$$0$$

Maple displays a vertical line at the asymptote, unless you specify discont=true.

```
> plot(expr, x=-5..5, y=-10..10);
```

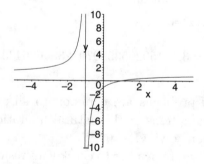

Maple removes the singularity $x = 1$ from the expression before solving it. Independent of the method or tools you use to solve equations, always check your results. These checks are easy to do in Maple.

3.3 Other Solvers

Maple contains a number of specialized solve commands. Since you are not as likely to find these as useful as the more general commands, `solve` and `fsolve`, this section only briefly mentions some of them. If you require more details on any of these commands, take advantage of the online help by entering ? and the command name at the Maple prompt.

Finding Integer Solutions

The `isolve` command finds integer solutions to equations, solving for all unknowns in the expression(s).

```
> isolve({3*x-4*y=7});
```

$$\{x = 5 + 4\_Z1, y = 2 + 3\_Z1\}$$

Maple uses the global names $\_Z1, \ldots, \_Zn$ to denote the integer parameters of the solution.

Finding Solutions Modulo m

The `msolve` command solves equations in the integers modulo m (the positive representation for integers), solving for all unknowns in the expression(s).

```
> msolve({3*x-4*y=1,7*x+y=2},17);
```

$$\{y = 6, x = 14\}$$

```
> msolve({2^n=3},19);
```

$$\{n = 13 + 18\_Z1^\sim\}$$

The tilde ($\sim$) on $\_Z1$ indicates that `msolve` has placed an assumption on $\_Z1$, in this case that $\_Z1$ is an integer.

```
> about( _Z1 );
```

```
Originally _Z1, renamed _Z1~:
  is assumed to be: integer
```

Section 5.2 describes how you can place assumptions on unknowns.

Solving Recurrence Relations

The `rsolve` command solves recurrence equations, returning an expression for the general term of the function.

```
> rsolve({f(n)=f(n-1)+f(n-2),f(0)=1,f(1)=1},{f(n)});
```

$$\left\{ f(n) = \frac{2}{5} \frac{\sqrt{5}\,(-\dfrac{2}{1+\sqrt{5}})^n}{1+\sqrt{5}} - \frac{2}{5} \frac{\sqrt{5}\,(-\dfrac{2}{1-\sqrt{5}})^n}{1-\sqrt{5}} \right\}$$

For more information, refer to **?LREtools**.

3.4   Polynomials

A *polynomial* in Maple is an expression containing unknowns. Each term in the polynomial contains a product of the unknowns. For example, should the polynomial contain only one unknown, x, then the terms might contain x^3, $x^1 = x$, and $x^0 = 1$ as in the case of the polynomial $x^3 - 2x + 1$. If more than one unknown exists, then a term may also contain a product of the unknowns, as in the polynomial $x^3 + 3x^2y + y^2$. Coefficients can be integers (as in the previous examples), rational numbers, irrational numbers, floating-point numbers, complex numbers, or other variables.

```
> x^2 - 1;
```

$$x^2 - 1$$

```
> x + y + z;
```

$$x + y + z$$

```
> 1/2*x^2 - sqrt(3)*x - 1/3;
```

$$\frac{1}{2}x^2 - \sqrt{3}\,x - \frac{1}{3}$$

```
> (1 - I)*x + 3 + 4*I;
```

$$(1 - I)\,x + 3 + 4\,I$$

```
> a*x^4 + b*x^3 + c*x^2 + d*x + f;
```

$$a\,x^4 + b\,x^3 + c\,x^2 + d\,x + f$$

Maple possesses commands for many kinds of manipulations and mathematical calculations with polynomials. The following sections investigate some of them.

Sorting and Collecting

The **sort** command arranges a polynomial into descending order of powers of the unknowns. Rather than making another copy of the polynomial with the terms in order, **sort** modifies the way Maple stores the original polynomial in memory. In other words, if you display your polynomial after sorting it, you will find that it retains the new order.

```
> sort_poly := x + x^2 - x^3 + 1 - x^4;
```

$$sort\_poly := x + x^2 - x^3 + 1 - x^4$$

```
> sort(sort_poly);
```

$$-x^4 - x^3 + x^2 + x + 1$$

```
> sort_poly;
```

$$-x^4 - x^3 + x^2 + x + 1$$

Maple sorts multivariate polynomials in two ways. The default method sorts them by total degree of the terms. Thus, x^2y^2 will come before both x^3 and y^3. The other option sorts by pure lexicographic order (**plex**). When you choose this option, the sort deals first with the powers of the first variable in the variable list (second argument) and then with the powers of the second variable. The difference between these sorts is best shown by an example.

```
> mul_var_poly := y^3 + x^2*y^2 + x^3;
```

$$mul\_var\_poly := y^3 + x^2\,y^2 + x^3$$

```
> sort(mul_var_poly, [x,y]);
```

$$x^2\,y^2 + x^3 + y^3$$

```
> sort(mul_var_poly, [x,y], 'plex');
```

$$x^3 + x^2\,y^2 + y^3$$

The `collect` command groups coefficients of like powers in a polynomial. For example, if the terms ax and bx are in a polynomial, Maple collects them as $(a + b)x$.

```
> big_poly:=x*y + z*x*y + y*x^2 - z*y*x^2 + x + z*x;
```

$$big\_poly := x\,y + z\,x\,y + y\,x^2 - z\,y\,x^2 + x + z\,x$$

```
> collect(big_poly, x);
```

$$(y - z\,y)\,x^2 + (y + z\,y + 1 + z)\,x$$

```
> collect(big_poly, z);
```

$$(x\,y - y\,x^2 + x)\,z + x\,y + y\,x^2 + x$$

Mathematical Operations

You can perform many mathematical operations on polynomials. Among the most fundamental is division, that is, to divide one polynomial into another and determine the quotient and remainder. Maple provides the commands `rem` and `quo` to find the remainder and quotient of a polynomial division.

```
> r := rem(x^3+x+1, x^2+x+1, x);
```

$$r := 2 + x$$

```
> q := quo(x^3+x+1, x^2+x+1, x);
```

$$q := x - 1$$

```
> collect( (x^2+x+1) * q + r, x );
```

$$x^3 + x + 1$$

On the other hand, sometimes it is sufficient to know whether one polynomial divides into another polynomial exactly. The **divide** command tests for exact polynomial division.

```
> divide(x^3 - y^3, x - y);
```

$$true$$

```
> rem(x^3 - y^3, x - y, x);
```

$$0$$

You evaluate polynomials at values as you would with any expression, by using **eval**.

```
> poly := x^2 + 3*x - 4;
```

$$poly := x^2 + 3\,x - 4$$

```
> eval(poly, x=2);
```

$$6$$

```
> mul_var_poly := y^2*x - 2*y + x^2*y + 1;
```

$$mul\_var\_poly := y^2\,x - 2\,y + y\,x^2 + 1$$

```
> eval(mul_var_poly, {y=1,x=-1});
```

$$-1$$

Table 3.1 Commands for Finding Polynomial Coefficients

Command	*Description*
coeff	extract coefficient
lcoeff	find the leading coefficient
tcoeff	find the trailing coefficient
coeffs	return a sequence of all the coefficients
degree	determine the (highest) degree of the polynomial
ldegree	determine the lowest degree of the polynomial

Coefficients and Degrees

The commands `degree` and `coeff` determine the degree of a polynomial and provide a mechanism for extracting coefficients.

```
> poly := 3*z^3 - z^2 + 2*z - 3*z + 1;
```

$$poly := 3\,z^3 - z^2 - z + 1$$

```
> coeff(poly, z^2);
```

$$-1$$

```
> degree(poly,z);
```

$$3$$

Root Finding and Factorization

The `solve` command determines the roots of a polynomial whereas the `factor` command expresses the polynomial in fully factored form.

```
> poly1 := x^6 - x^5 - 9*x^4 + x^3 + 20*x^2 + 12*x;
```

$$poly1 := x^6 - x^5 - 9\,x^4 + x^3 + 20\,x^2 + 12\,x$$

```
> factor(poly1);
```

$$x\,(x-2)\,(x-3)\,(x+2)\,(x+1)^2$$

```
> poly2 := (x + 3);
```

$$poly2 := x + 3$$

```
> poly3 := expand(poly2^6);
```

$$poly3 := $$
$$x^6 + 18\,x^5 + 135\,x^4 + 540\,x^3 + 1215\,x^2 + 1458\,x + 729$$

```
> factor(poly3);
```

$$(x + 3)^6$$

```
> solve({poly3=0}, {x});
```

$$\{x = -3\},\ \{x = -3\},\ \{x = -3\},\ \{x = -3\},\ \{x = -3\},\ \{x = -3\}$$

```
> factor(x^3 + y^3);
```

$$(x + y)\,(x^2 - x\,y + y^2)$$

Maple factors the polynomial over the ring implied by the coefficients (integers, rationals, etcetera). The **factor** command also allows you to specify an algebraic number field over which to factor the polynomial. For more information, refer to the help page **?factor**. For a list of functions that act on polynomials, see Table 3.2.

3.5   Calculus

Maple provides many powerful tools for solving problems in calculus, such as computing the limits of functions.

For example, compute the limit of a rational function as x approaches 1.

```
> f := x -> (x^2-2*x+1)/(x^4 + 3*x^3 - 7*x^2 + x+2);
```

$$f := x \to \frac{x^2 - 2\,x + 1}{x^4 + 3\,x^3 - 7\,x^2 + x + 2}$$

```
> Limit(f(x), x=1);
```

Table 3.2 Functions that Act on Polynomials

Function	Description
content	content of a multivariate polynomial
compoly	polynomial decomposition
discrim	discriminant of a polynomial
gcd	greatest common divisor
gcdex	extended Euclidean algorithm
interp	polynomial interpolation
lcm	least common multiple
norm	norm of a polynomial
prem	pseudo-remainder
primpart	primitive part of a multivariate polynomial
randpoly	random polynomial
recipoly	reciprocal polynomial
resultant	resultant of two polynomials
roots	roots over an algebraic number field
sqrfree	square-free factorization

$$\lim_{x \to 1} \frac{x^2 - 2x + 1}{x^4 + 3x^3 - 7x^2 + x + 2}$$

```
> value(%);
```

$$\frac{1}{8}$$

Taking the limit of an expression from either the positive or the negative direction is also possible. For example, consider the limit of $\tan(x)$ as x approaches $\pi/2$.

Calculate the left-hand limit by using the option left.

```
> Limit(tan(x), x=Pi/2, left);
```

$$\lim_{x \to (1/2\,\pi)-} \tan(x)$$

```
> value(%);
```

$$\infty$$

Do the same for the right-hand limit.

```
> Limit(tan(x), x=Pi/2, right);
```

$$\lim_{x \to (1/2\,\pi)+} \tan(x)$$

```
> value(%);
```

$$-\infty$$

Another operation easily performed in Maple is the creation of series approximations of a function. For example, use the function

```
> f := x -> sin(4*x)*cos(x);
```

$$f := x \to \sin(4\,x)\cos(x)$$

```
> fs1 := series(f(x), x=0);
```

$$fs1 := 4\,x - \frac{38}{3}\,x^3 + \frac{421}{30}\,x^5 + \mathrm{O}(x^6)$$

Note that, by default, the **series** command generates an order 6 polynomial. By changing the value of the special variable, **Order**, you can increase or decrease the order of a polynomial series.

Using **convert(fs1, polynom)** removes the order term from the series so that Maple can plot it.

```
> p := convert(fs1,polynom);
```

$$p := 4\,x - \frac{38}{3}\,x^3 + \frac{421}{30}\,x^5$$

```
> plot({f(x), p},x=-1..1, -2..2);
```

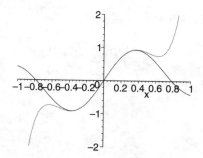

If you increase the order of truncation of the series to 12 and try again, you see the expected improvement in the accuracy of the approximation.

```
> Order := 12;
```

$$Order := 12$$

```
> fs1 := series(f(x), x=0);
```

$$fs1 := 4\,x - \frac{38}{3}\,x^3 + \frac{421}{30}\,x^5 - \frac{10039}{1260}\,x^7 + \frac{246601}{90720}\,x^9 - \frac{6125659}{9979200}\,x^{11} + O(x^{12})$$

```
> p := convert(fs1,polynom);
```

$$p := 4\,x - \frac{38}{3}\,x^3 + \frac{421}{30}\,x^5 - \frac{10039}{1260}\,x^7 + \frac{246601}{90720}\,x^9$$
$$- \frac{6125659}{9979200}\,x^{11}$$

```
> plot({f(x), p}, x=-1..1, -2..2);
```

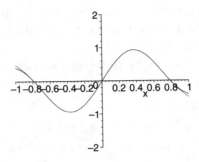

Maple can symbolically compute derivatives and integrals. For example, differentiate an expression, integrate its result, and compare it with the original expression.

```
> f := x -> x*sin(a*x) + b*x^2;
```

$$f := x \rightarrow x \sin(a\,x) + b\,x^2$$

```
> Diff(f(x),x);
```

$$\frac{\partial}{\partial x}\left(x \sin(a\,x) + b\,x^2\right)$$

```
> df := value(%);
```

$$df := \sin(a\,x) + x \cos(a\,x)\,a + 2\,b\,x$$

```
> Int(df, x);
```

$$\int \sin(a\,x) + x \cos(a\,x)\,a + 2\,b\,x\,dx$$

```
> value(%);
```

$$-\frac{\cos(a\,x)}{a} + \frac{\cos(a\,x) + a\,x \sin(a\,x)}{a} + b\,x^2$$

```
> simplify(%);
```

$$x\left(\sin(a\,x) + b\,x\right)$$

It is unnecessary to use the inert forms `Diff` and `Int` in conjunction with the `value` command to symbolically compute the derivative and integral, respectively. The results can be calculated in single commands by using `diff` and `int`, respectively.

You can also perform definite integrations. For example, recompute the previous integral on the interval $x = 1$ to $x = 2$.

```
> Int(df,x=1..2);
```

$$\int_1^2 \sin(a\,x) + x\cos(a\,x)\,a + 2\,b\,x\,dx$$

```
> value(%);
```

$$2\sin(2\,a) + 3\,b - \sin(a)$$

Consider a more complicated integral.

```
> Int(exp(-x^2), x);
```

$$\int e^{(-x^2)}\,dx$$

```
> value(%);
```

$$\frac{1}{2}\sqrt{\pi}\operatorname{erf}(x)$$

If Maple cannot clearly determine whether a variable is real or complex, it may return an unexpected result.

```
> g := t -> exp(-a*t)*ln(t);
```

$$g := t \to e^{(-a\,t)}\ln(t)$$

```
> Int (g(t), t=0..infinity);
```

$$\int_0^\infty e^{(-a\,t)}\ln(t)\,dt$$

```
> value(%);
```

$$\lim_{t\to\infty} -\frac{e^{(-a\,t)}\ln(t) + \mathrm{Ei}(1,\,a\,t) + \gamma + \ln(a)}{a}$$

Here Maple assumes that the parameter **a** is a complex number. Hence, it returns a more general answer.

For situations where you know that **a** is a positive, real number, indicate this by using the **assume** command.

```
> assume(a > 0):
> ans := Int(g(t), t=0..infinity);
```

$$ans := \int_0^\infty e^{(-a\tilde{\ }\,t)}\ln(t)\,dt$$

```
> value(%);
```

$$-\frac{\ln(a\tilde{\ })}{a\tilde{\ }} - \frac{\gamma}{a\tilde{\ }}$$

The result is much simpler. The only non-elementary term is the constant **gamma**. The tilde ($\tilde{\ }$) indicates that **a** carries an assumption. Remove the assumption to proceed to more examples. You must do this in two steps. The answer, **ans**, contains **a** with assumptions. If you want to reset and continue to use **ans**, then you must replace all occurrences of $a\tilde{\ }$ with a.

```
> ans := subs(a ='a', ans );
```

$$ans := \int_0^\infty e^{(-a\,t)}\ln(t)\,dt$$

The first argument, **a = 'a'**, deserves special attention. If you type a after making an assumption about a, Maple automatically assumes you mean $a\tilde{\ }$. In Maple, single quotes *delay evaluation*. In this case, they ensure that Maple interprets the second **a** as a and not as $a\tilde{\ }$.

Now that you have removed the assumption on **a** inside **ans**, you can remove the assumption on **a** itself by assigning it to its own name.

```
> a := 'a':
```

Use single quotes here to remove the assumption on **a**. For more information on assumptions, see section 5.2.

3.6   Differential Equations: `dsolve`

Maple can symbolically solve many ordinary differential equations (ODEs), including initial value and boundary value problems.

Define an ODE.

```
> ode1 := {diff(y(t),t,t) + 5*diff(y(t),t) + 6*y(t)  = 0};
```

$$ode1 := \{(\frac{d^2}{dt^2}\,y(t)) + 5\,(\frac{d}{dt}\,y(t)) + 6\,y(t) = 0\}$$

Define initial conditions.

```
> ic := {y(0)=0, D(y)(0)=1};
```

$$ic := \{y(0) = 0,\ D(y)(0) = 1\}$$

Solve with `dsolve`, using the `union` operator to form the union of the two sets.

```
> soln := dsolve(ode1 union ic, {y(t)});
```

$$soln := y(t) = -e^{(-3t)} + e^{(-2t)}$$

If you want to evaluate the solution at points or plot it, remember to use the `unapply` command to define a proper Maple function. For more information, see section 3.1.

You can conveniently extract a value from a solution set with the aid of `eval`.

```
> eval( y(t), soln );
```

$$-e^{(-3t)} + e^{(-2t)}$$

Use this fact to define y as a function of t using `unapply`:

```
> y1:= unapply(%, t );
```

$$y1 := t \rightarrow -e^{(-3t)} + e^{(-2t)}$$

```
> y1(a);
```

$$-e^{(-3a)} + e^{(-2a)}$$

Verify that y1 is indeed a solution to the ODE:

```
> eval(ode1, y=y1);
```

$$\{0 = 0\}$$

and that y1 satisfies the initial conditions.

```
> eval(ic, y=y1);
```

$$\{0 = 0,\ 1 = 1\}$$

Another method for solution checking is also available. Assign the new solution to y instead of y1.

```
> y := unapply( eval(y(t), soln), t );
```

$$y := t \rightarrow -e^{(-3t)} + e^{(-2t)}$$

Now when you enter an equation containing y, Maple uses this function and evaluates the result, all in one step.

```
> ode1;
```

$$\{0 = 0\}$$

```
> ic;
```

$$\{0 = 0,\ 1 = 1\}$$

If you want to change the differential equation, or the definition of $y(t)$, then you can remove the definition with the following command.

```
> y := 'y';
```

$$y := y$$

Maple also understands special functions, such as the Dirac delta or impulse function, used in physics.

```
> ode2 := 10^6*diff(y(x),x,x,x,x) = Dirac(x-2) -
>    Dirac(x-4);
```

$$ode2 := 1000000\,(\frac{d^4}{dx^4}\,\mathrm{y}(x)) = \mathrm{Dirac}(x - 2) - \mathrm{Dirac}(x - 4)$$

Specify boundary conditions

```
> bc := {y(0)=0, D(D(y))(0)=0, y(5)=0};
```

$$bc := \{\mathrm{y}(0) = 0,\ \mathrm{y}(5) = 0,\ (\mathrm{D}^{(2)})(y)(0) = 0\}$$

and an initial value.

```
> iv := {D(D(y))(5)=0};
```

$$iv := \{(\mathrm{D}^{(2)})(y)(5) = 0\}$$

```
> soln := dsolve({ode2} union bc union iv, {y(x)});
```

$$soln := \mathrm{y}(x) = \frac{1}{6000000}\,\mathrm{Heaviside}(x - 2)\,x^3$$

$$-\,\frac{1}{750000}\,\mathrm{Heaviside}(x - 2) + \frac{1}{500000}\,\mathrm{Heaviside}(x - 2)\,x$$

$$-\,\frac{1}{1000000}\,\mathrm{Heaviside}(x - 2)\,x^2$$

$$-\,\frac{1}{6000000}\,\mathrm{Heaviside}(x - 4)\,x^3 + \frac{1}{93750}\,\mathrm{Heaviside}(x - 4)$$

$$-\,\frac{1}{125000}\,\mathrm{Heaviside}(x - 4)\,x + \frac{1}{500000}\,\mathrm{Heaviside}(x - 4)\,x^2$$

$$-\,\frac{1}{15000000}\,x^3 + \frac{1}{1250000}\,x$$

```
> eval(y(x), soln);
```

$$\frac{1}{6000000}\,\text{Heaviside}(x-2)\,x^3 - \frac{1}{750000}\,\text{Heaviside}(x-2)$$

$$+\frac{1}{500000}\,\text{Heaviside}(x-2)\,x$$

$$-\frac{1}{1000000}\,\text{Heaviside}(x-2)\,x^2$$

$$-\frac{1}{6000000}\,\text{Heaviside}(x-4)\,x^3 + \frac{1}{93750}\,\text{Heaviside}(x-4)$$

$$-\frac{1}{125000}\,\text{Heaviside}(x-4)\,x + \frac{1}{500000}\,\text{Heaviside}(x-4)\,x^2$$

$$-\frac{1}{15000000}\,x^3 + \frac{1}{1250000}\,x$$

```
> y := unapply(%, x);
```

$$y := x \to \frac{1}{6000000}\,\text{Heaviside}(x-2)\,x^3$$

$$-\frac{1}{750000}\,\text{Heaviside}(x-2) + \frac{1}{500000}\,\text{Heaviside}(x-2)\,x$$

$$-\frac{1}{1000000}\,\text{Heaviside}(x-2)\,x^2$$

$$-\frac{1}{6000000}\,\text{Heaviside}(x-4)\,x^3 + \frac{1}{93750}\,\text{Heaviside}(x-4)$$

$$-\frac{1}{125000}\,\text{Heaviside}(x-4)\,x + \frac{1}{500000}\,\text{Heaviside}(x-4)\,x^2$$

$$-\frac{1}{15000000}\,x^3 + \frac{1}{1250000}\,x$$

This value of y satisfies the differential equation, the boundary conditions, and the initial value.

```
> ode2;
```

$$-6\,\mathrm{Dirac}(1,\,x-4)\,x + 6\,\mathrm{Dirac}(1,\,x-2)\,x - 12\,\mathrm{Dirac}(1,\,x-2)$$

$$+\frac{32}{3}\,\mathrm{Dirac}(3,\,x-4) - 8\,\mathrm{Dirac}(3,\,x-4)\,x$$

$$-\frac{1}{6}\,\mathrm{Dirac}(3,\,x-4)\,x^3 - \mathrm{Dirac}(3,\,x-2)\,x^2$$

$$+2\,\mathrm{Dirac}(3,\,x-2)\,x + \frac{1}{6}\,\mathrm{Dirac}(3,\,x-2)\,x^3$$

$$+2\,\mathrm{Dirac}(3,\,x-4)\,x^2 + 8\,\mathrm{Dirac}(2,\,x-2) - \frac{4}{3}\,\mathrm{Dirac}(3,\,x-2)$$

$$-32\,\mathrm{Dirac}(2,\,x-4) + 16\,\mathrm{Dirac}(2,\,x-4)\,x$$

$$+2\,\mathrm{Dirac}(2,\,x-2)\,x^2 - 8\,\mathrm{Dirac}(2,\,x-2)\,x$$

$$-2\,\mathrm{Dirac}(2,\,x-4)\,x^2 + 24\,\mathrm{Dirac}(1,\,x-4) + 4\,\mathrm{Dirac}(x-2)$$

$$-4\,\mathrm{Dirac}(x-4) = \mathrm{Dirac}(x-2) - \mathrm{Dirac}(x-4)$$

```
> simplify(%);
```

$$\mathrm{Dirac}(x-2) - \mathrm{Dirac}(x-4) = \mathrm{Dirac}(x-2) - \mathrm{Dirac}(x-4)$$

```
> bc;
```

$$\{0 = 0\}$$

```
> iv;
```

$$\{0 = 0\}$$

```
> plot(y(x), x=0..5, axes=BOXED);
```

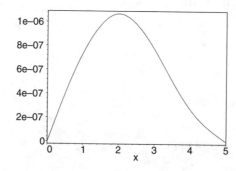

Unassign **y** now since you are done with it.

```
> y := 'y';
```

$$y := y$$

Maple can also solve systems of differential equations. For example, solve the following system of two simultaneous, second order equations.

```
> de_sys := { diff(y(x),x,x)=z(x), diff(z(x),x,x)=y(x) };
```

$$de\_sys := \{\frac{d^2}{dx^2}\, y(x) = z(x),\ \frac{d^2}{dx^2}\, z(x) = y(x)\}$$

```
> soln := dsolve(de_sys, {z(x),y(x)});
```

$$soln := \{y(x) = \_C1\ e^x + \_C2\ e^{(-x)} + \_C3\ \sin(x) + \_C4\ \cos(x),$$
$$z(x) = \_C1\ e^x + \_C2\ e^{(-x)} - \_C3\ \sin(x) - \_C4\ \cos(x)\}$$

If you solve the system without providing additional conditions, Maple automatically generates the appropriate constants $\_C1$, ..., $\_C4$.

Again, observe that you can easily extract and define the solutions with the aid of **eval** and **unapply**:

```
> y := unapply(eval(y(x), soln), x );
```

$$y := x \to \_C1\ e^x + \_C2\ e^{(-x)} + \_C3\ \sin(x) + \_C4\ \cos(x)$$

```
> y(1);
```

$$\_C1\ e + \_C2\ e^{(-1)} + \_C3\ \sin(1) + \_C4\ \cos(1)$$

and you can unassign it again when you are finished with it.

```
> y := 'y';
```

$$y := y$$

3.7   The Organization of Maple

When you start Maple, it loads only the *kernel*. The kernel is the base of Maple's system. It contains fundamental and primitive commands: the Maple language interpreter (which converts the commands you enter into machine instructions your computer processor can understand), algorithms for basic numerical calculation, and routines to display results and perform other input and output operations.

The kernel consists of highly optimized *C* code—approximately 10% of the system's total size. Maple programmers have deliberately kept the size of the kernel small for speed and efficiency. The Maple kernel implements the most frequently used routines for integer and rational arithmetic and simple polynomial calculations.

The remaining 90% of Maple's mathematical knowledge is written in the Maple language and resides in the Maple library. Maple's library divides into two groups: the *main* library and the packages. These groups of functions sit above the kernel.

The *main* library contains the most frequently used Maple commands (other than those in the kernel). These commands load upon demand— you do not need to explicitly load them. The Maple language produces very compact procedures that read with no observable delay, so you are not likely to notice which commands are C-coded kernel commands and which are loaded from the library.

The last commands in the library are in the packages. Each one of Maple's numerous packages contains a group of commands for related calculations. For example, the `LinearAlgebra` package contains commands for the manipulation of Matrices.

You can use a command from a package in three ways.

1. Use the complete name of the package and the desired command.

   > | *package* [*cmd*] (...) |

   If the package has a subpackage, use the complete name of the package, the complete name of the subpackage, and the desired command.

   > | *package* [*subpackage*] [*cmd*] (...) |

2. Activate the short names for all the commands in a package by using the `with` command.

```
with(package)
```

If the package has a subpackage, use the following **with** command.

```
with(package[subpackage])
```

Then use the short name for the command.

```
cmd(...)
```

3. Activate the short name for a single command from a package.

```
with(package, cmd)
```

If the package has a subpackage, use the following command.

```
with(package[subpackage], cmd)
```

Then use the short form of the command name.

```
cmd(...)
```

This next example uses the **Tangent** command in the **Student** package to calculate the slope of the tangent of the expression $sin(x)$ at the point $x = 0$.

```
> with(Student[Calculus1]);
```

> [*AntiderivativePlot, ApproximateInt, ArcLength,*
> *Asymptotes, Clear, CriticalPoints, DerivativePlot,*
> *ExtremePoints, FunctionAverage, FunctionChart,*
> *GetMessage, GetNumProblems, GetProblem, Hint,*
> *InflectionPoints, Integrand, InversePlot,*
> *MeanValueTheorem, NewtonQuotient, NewtonsMethod,*
> *PointInterpolation, RiemannSum, RollesTheorem,*
> *Roots, Rule, Show, ShowIncomplete, ShowSteps,*
> *Summand, SurfaceOfRevolution, Tangent,*
> *TaylorApproximation, Understand, Undo,*
> *VolumeOfRevolution, WhatProblem*]

```
> Tangent(sin(x), x = 0);
```

$$x$$

When you enter with(*package*);, you see a list of all the short names of the commands in the package. Plus, Maple warns you if it has redefined any pre-existing names.

3.8   The Maple Packages

Maple's built-in packages of specialized commands perform tasks from an extensive variety of disciplines, from Student Calculus to General Relativity Theory. The examples in this section are not intended to be comprehensive. They are simply examples of a few commands in selected packages, to give you a glimpse of Maple's functionality.

List of Packages

The following list of packages can also be found by reading the help page ?packages. For a full list of commands in a particular package, refer to the help page, ?*packagename*.

algcurves tools for studying the one-dimensional algebraic varieties (curves) defined by multi-variate polynomials.

codegen tools for creating, manipulating, and translating Maple procedures into other languages. Includes automatic differentiation, code optimization, translation into languages such as C and Fortran.

CodeGeneration functions that translate Maple code to other programming languages, including Java.

combinat combinatorial functions, including commands for calculating permutations and combinations of lists, and partitions of integers. (Use the combstruct package instead, where possible.)

combstruct commands for generating and counting combinatorial structures, as well as determining generating function equations for such counting.

context tools for building and modifying context-sensitive menus in Maple's graphical user interface (for example, when right-clicking on an output expression).

CurveFitting commands that support curve-fitting.

DEtools tools for manipulating, solving, and plotting systems of differential equations, phase portraits, and field plots.

diffalg commands for manipulating systems of differential polynomial equations (ODEs or PDEs).

difforms commands for handling differential forms; for problems in differential geometry.

Domains commands to create *domains of computation*; supports computing with polynomials, matrices, and series over number rings, finite fields, polynomial rings, and matrix rings.

ExternalCalling commands that link to external functions.

finance commands for financial computations.

GaussInt commands for working with Gaussian Integers; that is, numbers of the form $a + bI$ where a and b are integers. Commands for finding GCDs, factoring, and primality testing.

genfunc commands for manipulating rational generating functions.

geom3d commands for three-dimensional Euclidean geometry; to define and manipulate points, lines, planes, triangles, spheres, polyhedra, etcetera, in three dimensions.

geometry commands for two-dimensional Euclidean geometry; to define and manipulate points, lines, triangles, and circles in two dimensions.

Groebner commands for Gröbner basis computations; in particular tools for Ore algebras and D-modules.

group commands for working with permutation groups and finitely-presented groups.

inttrans commands for working with integral transforms and their inverses.

LibraryTools commands for library manipulation and processing.

liesymm commands for characterizing the contact symmetries of systems of partial differential equations.

linalg over 100 commands for matrix and vector manipulation; everything from adding two matrices to symbolic eigenvectors and eigenvalues.

LinearAlgebra enhanced linear algebra commands for creating special types of Matrices, calculating with large numeric Matrices, and performing Matrix algebra.

LinearFunctionalSystems commands that solve linear functional systems with polynomial coefficients, find the universal denominator of a rational solution, and transform a matrix recurrence system into an equivalent system with a nonsingular leading or trailing matrix.

ListTools commands that manipulate lists.

LREtools commands for manipulating, plotting, and solving linear recurrence equations.

Maplets commands for creating windows, dialogs, and other visual interfaces that interact with a user to provide the power of Maple.

MathML commands that import and export Maple expressions to and from MathML text.

Matlab commands to use several of Matlab's numerical matrix functions, including eigenvalues and eigenvectors, determinants, and LU-decomposition. (Only accessible if Matlab is installed on your system.)

MatrixPolynomialAlgebra set of tools for the algebraic manipulation of matrix polynomials.

networks tools for constructing, drawing, and analyzing combinatorial networks. Facilities for handling directed graphs, and arbitrary expressions for edge and vertex weights.

numapprox commands for calculating polynomial approximations to functions on a given interval.

numtheory commands for classic number theory, primality testing, finding the nth prime, factoring integers, generating cyclotomic polynomials. This package also contains commands for handling convergents.

Ore_algebra routines for basic computations in algebras of linear operators.

OrthogonalSeries commands for manipulating series of classical orthogonal polynomials or, more generally, hypergeometric polynomials.

orthopoly commands for generating various types of orthogonal polynomials; useful in differential equation solving.

padic commands for computing p-adic approximations to real numbers.

PDEtools tools for manipulating, solving and plotting partial differential equations.

plots commands for different types of specialized plots, including contour plots, two- and three-dimensional implicit plotting, plotting text, and plots in different coordinate systems.

plottools commands for generating and manipulating graphical objects.

PolynomialTools commands for manipulating polynomial objects.

powseries commands to create and manipulate formal power series represented in general form.

process the commands in this package allow you to write multi-process Maple programs under UNIX.

RandomTools commands for working with random objects.

RationalNormalForms commands that construct the polynomial normal form or rational canonical forms of a rational function, or minimal representation of a hypergeometric term.

RealDomain provides an environment in which the assumed underlying number system is the real number system not the complex number system.

ScientificConstants commands that provide access to the values of various constant physical quantities that occur in fields such as chemistry and physics.

simplex commands for linear optimization using the simplex algorithm.

Slode commands for finding formal power series solutions of linear ODEs.

Sockets commands for network communication in Maple. The routines in this package enable you to connect to processes on remote hosts on a network (such as an Intranet or the Internet) and exchange data with these processes.

SolveTools commands that solve systems of algebraic equations. This package gives expert users access to the routines used by the `solve` command for greater control over the solution process.

Spread tools for working with spreadsheets in Maple.

stats simple statistical manipulation of data; includes averaging, standard deviation, correlation coefficients, variance, and regression analysis.

StringTools optimized commands for string manipulation.

Student subpackages that are course specific. In future releases this package will be expanded to include other course specific subpackages. The first such subpackage is `Calculus1`.

> **Calculus1** commands for stepping through differentiation, integration, and limit problems, visualization of Newton's method, Riemann sums, arc length, volume of rotation and others, as well as routines for finding points of interest of an expression.

sumtools commands for computing indefinite and definite sums. Includes Gosper's algorithm and Zeilberger's algorithm.

SumTools tools for finding closed forms of definite and indefinite sums.

tensor commands for calculating with tensors and their applications in General Relativity Theory.

TypeTools commands for extending the set of recognized types in the type command.

Units commands for converting values between units, and environments for performing calculations with units.

VariationalCalculus commands for Calculus of Variations computations.

VectorCalculus procedures to perform multivariate and Vector calculus operations on objects based on the rtable datatype.

Worksheet commands that provide an infrastructure for generating and manipulating Maple worksheets by using the Maple language.

XMLTools commands that manipulate Maple's internal representation of XML documents.

The Student Calculus1 Package (Single Variable)

The Student[Calculus1] package helps you step through differentiation, integration, and limit calculus computations. As an example, consider this problem: Given the function $4 * x^2$, find its derivative.

```
> with(Student[Calculus1]):
> infolevel[Student] := 1:
```

To view a list of all the commands that Maple is loading, replace the colon at the end of the command with a semicolon.

```
> Diff(4*x^2, x);
```

$$\frac{d}{dx}\left(4\,x^2\right)$$

Use the constantmultiple rule.

```
> Rule[constantmultiple](%);
```

Creating problem #1

$$\frac{d}{dx}\left(4\,x^2\right) = 4\left(\frac{d}{dx}\left(x^2\right)\right)$$

Use the power rule.

```
> Rule[power](%);
```

$$\frac{d}{dx}\left(4\,x^2\right) = 8\,x$$

Consider the following integration example. Integrate $x * cos(x) + x$ from $x = 0$ to $x = \pi$.

```
> Int(x*cos(x) + x, x=0..Pi);
```

$$\int_0^\pi x\cos(x) + x\,dx$$

Use the sum rule.

```
> Rule[sum](%);
```

Creating problem #2

$$\int_0^\pi x\cos(x) + x\,dx = \int_0^\pi x\cos(x)\,dx + \int_0^\pi x\,dx$$

Use the **power** rule.

> Rule[power](%);

$$\int_0^\pi x\cos(x) + x\,dx = \int_0^\pi x\cos(x)\,dx + \frac{1}{2}\pi^2$$

Use the **Hint** command to determine a possible next step for the problem.

> Hint(%);

$$[parts,\ x,\ \sin(x)]$$

Use the hint with the **Rule** command.

> Rule[%](%%);

$$\int_0^\pi x\cos(x) + x\,dx = -\int_0^\pi \sin(x)\,dx + \frac{1}{2}\pi^2$$

Use the **sin** rule to complete this computation.

> Rule[sin](%);

$$\int_0^\pi x\cos(x) + x\,dx = -2 + \frac{1}{2}\pi^2$$

Use the **Student[Calculus1]** package to calculate the limit of $(1 + 1/x)^x$.

Use the **Understand** command to use rules for calculating the **Limit** without explicitly applying them. **Understand** the constant, constant multiple, power, and sum **Limit** rules for the following example.

> Understand(Limit, constant, 'c*', power, sum);

$$Limit = [constant,\ constantmultiple,\ power,\ sum]$$

```
> Limit((1 + 1/x)^x, x=infinity);
```

$$\lim_{x \to \infty} \left(1 + \frac{1}{x}\right)^x$$

Request a hint for the next step of the computation.

```
> Hint(%);
```

```
Creating problem #3
```

```
Rewrite the expression as an exponential to prepare for
using l'Hopital's rule
```

$$\left[rewrite, \left(1 + \frac{1}{x}\right)^x = e^{\left(x \ln\left(1 + \frac{1}{x}\right)\right)}\right]$$

Use the rule that is returned by Hint.

```
> Rule[%](%%);
```

$$\lim_{x \to \infty} \left(1 + \frac{1}{x}\right)^x = \lim_{x \to \infty} e^{\left(x \ln\left(1 + \frac{1}{x}\right)\right)}$$

```
> Hint(%);
```

$$[\exp]$$

```
> Rule[%](%%);
```

$$\lim_{x \to \infty} \left(1 + \frac{1}{x}\right)^x = e^{\left(\lim_{x \to \infty} x \ln\left(1 + \frac{1}{x}\right)\right)}$$

```
> Hint(%);
```

$$\left[lhopital, \ln\left(1 + \frac{1}{x}\right)\right]$$

```
> Rule[%](%%);
```

$$\lim_{x \to \infty} \left(1 + \frac{1}{x}\right)^x = e^{\left(\lim_{x \to \infty} \frac{x}{x+1}\right)}$$

```
> Hint(%);
```

$$\left[rewrite, \ \frac{x}{x+1} = \frac{1}{1 + \dfrac{1}{x}} \right]$$

```
> Rule[%](%%);
```

$$\lim_{x \to \infty} (1 + \frac{1}{x})^x = e$$

Consider the function $-2/3 * x^2 + x$. Plot the function and its tangent line at $x = 0$.

```
> Tangent(-2/3*x^2+x, x=0, -2..2, output=plot,
>           showtangent=true);
```

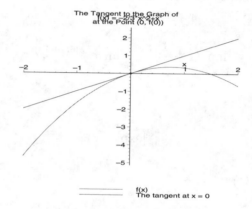

The Tangent to the Graph of
$f(x) = -2/3 \cdot x^2 + x$
at the Point $(0, f(0))$

—————— f(x)
The tangent at x = 0

Where does this curve cross the x-axis?

```
> Roots(-2/3*x^2+x);
```

$$[0, \frac{3}{2}]$$

You can find the area under the curve between these two points by using Riemann sums.

```
> ApproximateInt(-2/3*x^2+x, x=0..3/2, method=midpoint,
>                output=plot, view=[0..1.6, -0.15..0.4]);
```

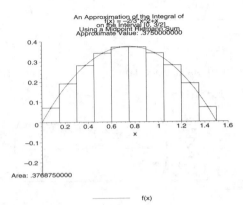

Since the result is not a good approximation, increase the number of boxes used to forty.

```
> ApproximateInt(-2/3*x^2+x, x=0..3/2, method=midpoint,
>                output=plot, view=[0..1.6, -0.15..0.4],
>                partition=40);
```

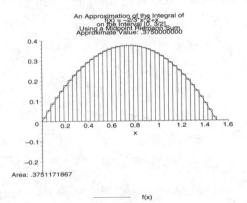

What is the actual value? First, use n boxes and output the sum formula.

```
> ApproximateInt(-2/3*x^2+x, x=0..3/2, method=midpoint,
>                output=sum, partition=n);
```

$$\frac{3}{2} \frac{\displaystyle\sum_{i=0}^{n-1} \left(-\frac{3}{2} \frac{(i+\frac{1}{2})^2}{n^2} + \frac{3}{2} \frac{i+\frac{1}{2}}{n} \right)}{n}$$

Then take the limit as n goes to ∞.

> Limit(%, n=infinity);

$$\lim_{n \to \infty} \frac{3}{2} \frac{\displaystyle\sum_{i=0}^{n-1} \left(-\frac{3}{2} \frac{(i+\frac{1}{2})^2}{n^2} + \frac{3}{2} \frac{i+\frac{1}{2}}{n} \right)}{n}$$

> value(%);

$$\frac{3}{8}$$

Now, observe that you can obtain the same result by using an integral.

> Int(-2/3*x^2+x, x=0..3/2);

$$\int_0^{3/2} -\frac{2}{3}x^2 + x \, dx$$

> value(%);

$$\frac{3}{8}$$

For more information on calculus with Maple, see chapter 6.

The LinearAlgebra Package

In linear algebra, a set of linearly independent vectors that generates the vector space is a basis. That is, you can uniquely express any element in the vector space as a linear combination of the elements of the basis.

A set of vectors $\{v_1, v_2, v_3, \ldots, v_n\}$ is linearly independent if and only if whenever

$$c_1 v_1 + c_2 v_2 + c_3 v_3 + \cdots + c_n v_n = 0$$

then

$$c_1 = c_2 = c_3 = \cdots = c_n = 0.$$

Problem: Determine a basis for the vector space generated by the vectors $[1, -1, 0, 1]$, $[5, -2, 3, -1]$, and $[6, -3, 3, 0]$. Express the vector $[1, 2, 3, -5]$ with respect to this basis.

Solution: Enter the vectors.

```
> with(LinearAlgebra):
> v1:=<1|-1|0|1>:
> v2:=<5|-2|3|-1>:
> v3:=<6|-3|3|0>:
> vector_space:=<v1,v2,v3>;
```

$$vector\_space := \begin{bmatrix} 1 & -1 & 0 & 1 \\ 5 & -2 & 3 & -1 \\ 6 & -3 & 3 & 0 \end{bmatrix}$$

If the vectors are linearly independent, then they form a basis. To test linear independence, set up the equation $c_1 v_1 + c_2 v_2 + c_3 v_3 = 0$

$$c_1[1, -1, 0, 1] + c_2[5, -2, 3, -1] + c_3[6, -3, 3, 0] = [0, 0, 0, 0]$$

which is equivalent to

$$
\begin{aligned}
c_1 + 5c_2 + 6c_3 &= 0 \\
-c_1 - 2c_2 - 3c_3 &= 0 \\
3c_2 + 3c_3 &= 0 \\
c_1 - c_2 &= 0
\end{aligned}
$$

```
> LinearSolve( Transpose(vector_space), <0,0,0,0> );
```

$$\begin{bmatrix} -\_t0_3 \\ -\_t0_3 \\ \_t0_3 \end{bmatrix}$$

The vectors are linearly dependent since each is a linear product of a variable. Thus, they cannot form a basis. The **RowSpace** command returns a basis for the vector space.

```
> b:=RowSpace(vector_space);
```

$$b := [[1, 0, 1, -1], [0, 1, 1, -2]]$$

```
> b1:=b[1]; b2:=b[2];
```

$$b1 := [1, 0, 1, -1]$$

$$b2 := [0, 1, 1, -2]$$

```
> basis:=<b1,b2>;
```

$$basis := \begin{bmatrix} 1 & 0 & 1 & -1 \\ 0 & 1 & 1 & -2 \end{bmatrix}$$

Express $[1, 2, 3, -5]$ in coordinates with respect to this basis.

```
> LinearSolve( Transpose(basis), <1|2|3|-5> );
```

$$\begin{bmatrix} 1 \\ 2 \end{bmatrix}$$

You can find further information on this package in the ?LinearAlgebra help page.

The Matlab Package

The Matlab package enables you to call selected MATLAB functions from a Maple session, provided you have MATLAB installed on your system.[1] MATLAB is an abbreviation of **mat**rix **lab**oratory and is a popular numerical computation package, used extensively by engineers and other computing professionals.

To enable the connection between the two products, first establish the connection between the two products by entering the command

```
> with(Matlab):
```

The call to the Matlab library automatically executes the openlink command.

To determine the eigenvalues and eigenvectors of a matrix of integers, first define the matrix in Maple syntax.

---

[1]There is also a *Symbolic Computation Toolbox* available for MATLAB that allows you to call Maple commands from MATLAB.

```
> A := Matrix([[1,2,3],[1,2,3],[2,5,6]]):
```

Then the following call to **eig** is made.

```
> P,W := eig(A, eigenvectors=true):
```

Notice what is to the left of the assignment operator. The (P,W) specifies that *two* outputs are to be generated and assigned to variables — the eigenvalues to W and the eigenvectors to P. This multiple assignment is available to standard Maple commands but, since existing Maple commands are designed to create a single result, is rarely used.

Consider the individual results.

```
> W;
```

$$\begin{bmatrix} 9.321825 & 0. & 0. \\ 0. & -.5612673 \ 10^{-15} & 0. \\ 0. & 0. & -.3218253 \end{bmatrix}$$

```
> P;
```

$$\begin{bmatrix} -.3940365889964673 & -.9486832980505138 & -.5567547110202646 \\ -.3940365889964672 & -2.758331802155925 \ 10^{-16} & -.5567547110202655 \\ -.8303435030540421 & .3162277660168383 & .6164806432593667 \end{bmatrix}$$

The commands in this package can also take input in MATLAB format. Refer to the help page **?Matlab** for more information on acceptable input.

The Statistics Package

The **stats** package has many commands for data analysis and manipulation, and various types of statistical plotting. It also contains a wide range of statistical distributions.

The **stats** package contains subpackages. Within each subpackage, the commands are grouped by functionality.

```
> with(stats);
```

$$[anova, \ describe, \ fit, \ importdata, \ random, \ statevalf,$$
$$statplots, \ transform]$$

The **stats** package works with data in *statistical lists*, which can be standard Maple lists. A statistical list can also contain ranges and weighted values. The difference is best shown using an example. The name **marks** is assigned a standard list,

```
> marks :=
> [64,93,75,81,45,68,72,82,76,73];
```

$$marks := [64, 93, 75, 81, 45, 68, 72, 82, 76, 73]$$

as is **readings**

```
> readings := [ 0.75, 0.75, .003, 1.01, .9125,
>                .04, .83, 1.01, .874, .002 ];
```

$$readings := [0.75, 0.75, 0.003, 1.01, 0.9125, 0.04, 0.83,$$
$$1.01, 0.874, 0.002]$$

which is equivalent to the following statistical list.

```
> readings := [ Weight(.75, 2), .003, Weight(1.01, 2),
>                .9125, .04, .83, .874, .002 ];
```

$$readings := [Weight(0.75, 2), 0.003, Weight(1.01, 2),$$
$$0.9125, 0.04, 0.83, 0.874, 0.002]$$

The expression **Weight(x,n)** indicates that the value x appears n times in the list.

If differences less than 0.01 are so small that they are not meaningful, you can group them together, and simply give a range (using "..").

```
> readings := [ Weight(.75, 2), Weight(1.01, 2), .9125,
>                .04, .83, .874, Weight(0.002..0.003, 2) ];
```

$$readings := [Weight(0.75, 2), Weight(1.01, 2), 0.9125,$$
$$0.04, 0.83, 0.874, Weight(0.002..0.003, 2)]$$

The **describe** subpackage contains commands for data analysis.

```
> describe[mean](marks);
```

$$\frac{729}{10}$$

```
> describe[range](marks);
```

$$45..93$$

```
> describe[range](readings);
```

$$0.002..1.01$$

```
> describe[standarddeviation](readings);
```

$$0.4038750457$$

This package contains many statistical distributions. Generate some random data using the normal distribution, group it into ranges, and then plot a histogram of the ranges.

```
> random_data:=[random[normald](50)];
```

$$
\begin{aligned}
random\_data := [&0.1529160443,\ 0.7487697029, \\
&-0.4908898750,\ -0.6385850228,\ 0.7648245898, \\
&-0.04721150696,\ -1.463572278,\ 0.4470293004, \\
&1.342701867,\ 2.162605068,\ -0.2620109124, \\
&0.1093403084,\ -0.9886372087,\ -0.7765483851, \\
&-0.1231141571,\ 0.3876183720,\ 1.625165927, \\
&1.095665255,\ -0.2068680316,\ -1.283733823, \\
&1.583279600,\ 0.3045008349,\ -0.7304597374, \\
&0.4996033128,\ 0.8670709448,\ -0.1729739933, \\
&-0.6819890237,\ 0.005183053789,\ 0.8876933468, \\
&-0.3758638317,\ 1.452138520,\ 2.858250470, \\
&0.6917100232,\ 0.6341448687,\ 0.6707087107, \\
&0.5872984199,\ 0.03801888006,\ -0.1238893314, \\
&-0.01231563388,\ -0.7709242575,\ -1.599692668, \\
&0.8181350112,\ 0.08547526754,\ 0.09467224460, \\
&-1.407989130,\ 0.4128440679,\ -0.9586605355, \\
&-0.08180943597,\ 1.216070238,\ 0.5880450332]
\end{aligned}
$$

```
> ranges:=[-5..-2,-2..-1,-1..0,0..1,1..2,2..5];
```

$$ranges := [-5..-2,\ -2..-1,\ -1..0,\ 0..1,\ 1..2,\ 2..5]$$

```
> data_list:=transform[tallyinto](random_data,ranges);
```

$$data\_list := [\text{Weight}(-1..0, 17), \text{Weight}(0..1, 21),$$
$$\text{Weight}(2..5, 2), \text{Weight}(1..2, 6), \text{Weight}(-5.. - 2, 0),$$
$$\text{Weight}(-2.. - 1, 4)]$$

```
> statplots[histogram](data_list);
```

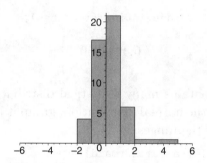

The Linear Optimization Package

The `simplex` package contains commands for linear optimization, using the simplex algorithm. Linear optimization involves finding optimal solutions to equations under constraints.

An example of a classic optimization problem is the pizza delivery problem. You have four pizzas to deliver, to four different places, spread throughout the city. You want to deliver all four using as little gas as possible. You also must get to all four locations in under twenty minutes, so that the pizzas stay hot. If you can create mathematical equations representing the routes to the four places and the distances, you can find the optimal solution. That is, you can determine what route you should take to get to all four places in as little time and using as little gas as possible. The constraints on this particular system are that you have to deliver all four pizzas within twenty minutes of leaving the restaurant.

Here is a very small system as an example.

```
> with(simplex);
```

```
Warning, the name basis has been redefined
Warning, the protected names maximize and minimize have
been redefined and unprotected
```

[*basis, convexhull, cterm, define_zero, display, dual,*
feasible, maximize, minimize, pivot, pivoteqn, pivotvar,
ratio, setup, standardize]

Say you want to maximize the expression w

```
> w   := -x+y+2*z;
```

$$w := -x + y + 2\,z$$

subject to the constraints c1, c2, and c3.

```
> c1 := 3*x+4*y-3*z    <= 23;
```

$$c1 := 3\,x + 4\,y - 3\,z \leq 23$$

```
> c2 := 5*x-4*y-3*z    <= 10;
```

$$c2 := 5\,x - 4\,y - 3\,z \leq 10$$

```
> c3 := 7*x +4*y+11*z <= 30;
```

$$c3 := 7\,x + 4\,y + 11\,z \leq 30$$

```
> maximize(w, {c1,c2,c3});
```

In this case, no answer means that Maple cannot find a solution. You can use the **feasible** command to determine if the set of constraints is valid.

```
> feasible({c1,c2,c3});
```

$$true$$

Try again, but this time place an additional restriction on the solution.

```
> maximize(w, {c1,c2,c3}, NONNEGATIVE);
```

$$\{z = \frac{1}{2},\, y = \frac{49}{8},\, x = 0\}$$

3.9 Conclusion

This chapter encompasses fundamental Maple features that will assist you greatly as you learn more complicated problem-solving methods. Section 3.1 introduced you to `solve` and `fsolve`, and how to properly use them. These methods will be useful time and again.

The final sections of this chapter introduced manipulations, `dsolve`, and the organization of Maple and the Maple library, in an attempt to give you a glimpse of Maple's potential.

4   Graphics

Sometimes the best way to get a better understanding of a mathematical structure is to graph it. Maple can produce several forms of graphs. For instance, some of its plotting capabilities include two-dimensional, three-dimensional, and animated graphs that you can view from any angle. Maple accepts explicit, implicit, and parametric forms, and recognizes many coordinate systems. Maple's flexibility allows you to easily manipulate graphs in many situations.

4.1   Graphing in Two Dimensions

When plotting an explicit function, $y = f(x)$, Maple requires the function and the domain.

```
> plot( sin(x), x=-2*Pi..2*Pi );
```

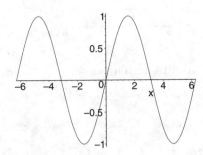

Clicking any point in the plot window shows those particular coordinates of the plot. The menus (found on the menubar or by right-clicking the plot itself) allow you to modify various characteristics of the plots or use many of the plotting command options listed under `?plot,options`. Maple can also graph user-defined functions.

```
> f := x -> 7*sin(x) + sin(7*x);
```

$$f := x \rightarrow 7\sin(x) + \sin(7x)$$

```
> plot(f(x), x=0..10);
```

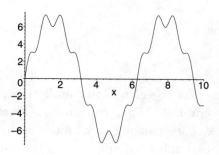

Maple allows you to focus on a specified section in the x- and y-dimensions.

```
> plot(f(x), x=0..10, y=4..8);
```

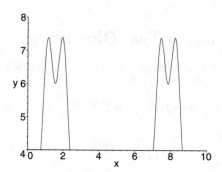

Maple can plot infinite domains.

```
> plot( sin(x)/x, x=0..infinity);
```

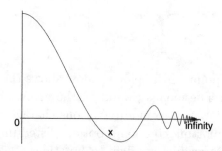

Parametric Plots

You cannot specify some graphs explicitly. In other words, you cannot write the dependent variable as a function, $y = f(x)$. For example, on a circle most x values correspond to two y values. One solution is to make both the x-coordinate and the y-coordinate functions of some parameter, for example, t. The graph generated from these functions is called a *parametric* plot. Use this syntax to specify parametric plots.

```
plot( [ x-expr, y-expr, parameter=range ] )
```

That is, you plot a list containing the *x-expr*, the *y-expr*, and the name and range of the parameter. For example

```
> plot( [ t^2, t^3, t=-1..1 ] );
```

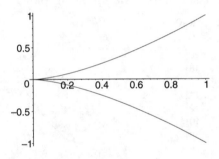

The points $(\cos t, \sin t)$ lie on a circle.

```
> plot( [ cos(t), sin(t), t=0..2*Pi ] );
```

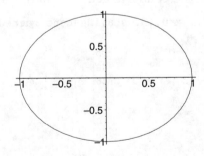

Rather than looking like a circle, the above plot resembles an ellipse because Maple, by default, scales the plot to fit the window. Here is the same plot again but with **scaling=constrained.**You can change the scaling by using the menus or the **scaling** option.

```
> plot( [ cos(t), sin(t), t=0..2*Pi ], scaling=constrained );
```

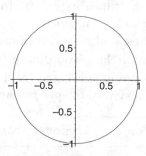

The drawback of **constrained scaling** is that it may obscure important details when the features in one dimension occur on a much smaller or larger scale than the others. The following plot is **unconstrained**.

```
> plot( exp(x), x=0..3 );
```

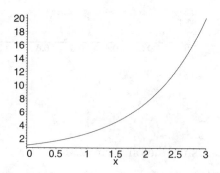

The following is the **constrained** version of the same plot.

```
> plot( exp(x), x=0..3, scaling=constrained);
```

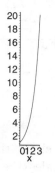

Polar Coordinates

Cartesian (ordinary) coordinates is the Maple default and is one among many ways of specifying a point in the plane. Polar coordinates, (r, θ), can also be used.

In polar coordinates, r is the distance from the origin to the point, while θ is the angle, measured in the counterclockwise direction, between the x-axis and the line through the origin and the point.

Maple can plot a function in polar coordinates by using the `polarplot` command. To access the short form of this command, you must first employ the `with(plots)` command.

```
> with(plots):
```

Figure 4.1 The Polar Coordinate System

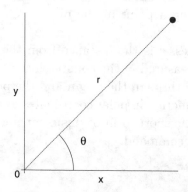

Use the following syntax to plot graphs in polar coordinates.

```
polarplot( r-expr, angle=range )
```

In polar coordinates, you can specify the circle explicitly, namely as $r = 1$.

```
> polarplot( 1, theta=0..2*Pi, scaling=constrained );
```

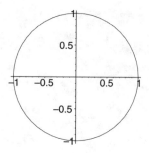

Use the `scaling=constrained` option to make the circle appear round. Here is the graph of $r = \sin(3\theta)$.

```
> polarplot( sin(3*theta), theta=0..2*Pi );
```

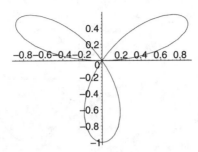

The graph of $r = \theta$ is a spiral.

```
> polarplot(theta, theta=0..4*Pi);
```

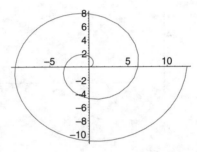

The `polarplot` command also accepts parametrized plots. That is, you can express the radius- and angle-coordinates in terms of a parameter, for example, t. The syntax is similar to a parametrized plot in Cartesian (ordinary) coordinates. See this section, page 99.

```
polarplot( [ r-expr, angle-expr, parameter=range ] )
```

The equations $r = \sin(t)$ and $\theta = \cos(t)$ define the following graph.

```
> polarplot( [ sin(t), cos(t), t=0..2*Pi ] );
```

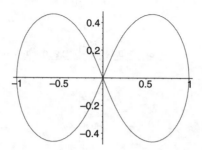

Here is the graph of $\theta = \sin(3r)$.

```
> polarplot( [ r, sin(3*r), r=0..7 ] );
```

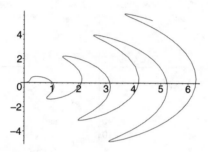

Functions with Discontinuities

Functions with discontinuities require extra attention. This function has two discontinuities, at $x = 1$ and at $x = 2$.

$$f(x) = \begin{cases} -1 & \text{if } x < 1, \\ 1 & \text{if } 1 \le x < 2, \\ 3 & \text{otherwise.} \end{cases}$$

Here is how to define $f(x)$ in Maple.

```
> f := x -> piecewise( x<1, -1, x<2, 1, 3 );
```

$$f := x \rightarrow \text{piecewise}(x < 1, -1, x < 2, 1, 3)$$

```
> plot(f(x), x=0..3);
```

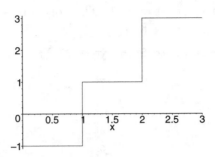

Maple draws almost vertical lines near the point of a discontinuity. The option **discont=true** indicates that there may be discontinuities.

```
> plot(f(x), x=0..3, discont=true);
```

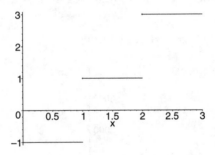

Functions with singularities, that is, those functions which become arbitrarily large at some point, constitute another special case. The function $x \mapsto 1/(x-1)^2$ has a singularity at $x = 1$.

```
> plot( 1/(x-1)^2, x=-5..6 );
```

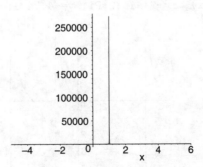

In the previous plot, all the interesting details of the graph are lost because there is a spike at $x = 1$. The solution is to view a narrower range, perhaps from $y = -1$ to 7.

```
> plot( 1/(x-1)^2, x=-5..6, y=-1..7 );
```

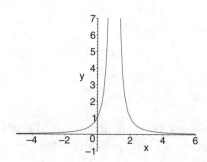

The tangent function has singularities at $x = \frac{\pi}{2} + \pi n$, where n is any integer.

```
> plot( tan(x), x=-2*Pi..2*Pi );
```

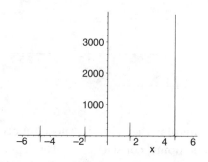

To see the details, reduce the range to $y = -4$ to 4.

```
> plot( tan(x), x=-2*Pi..2*Pi, y=-4..4 );
```

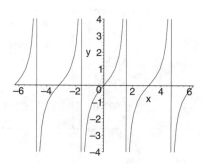

Maple draws almost vertical lines at the singularities, so you should use the `discont=true` option.

```
> plot( tan(x), x=-2*Pi..2*Pi, y=-4..4, discont=true );
```

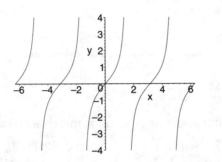

Multiple Functions

To graph more than one function in the same plot, give **plot** a list of functions.

```
> plot( [ x, x^2, x^3, x^4 ], x=-10..10, y=-10..10 );
```

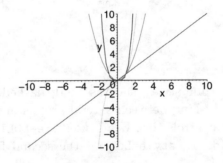

```
> f := x -> piecewise( x<0, cos(x), x>=0, 1+x^2 );
```

$$f := x \rightarrow \text{piecewise}(x < 0, \cos(x), 0 \le x, 1 + x^2)$$

```
> plot( [ f(x), diff(f(x), x), diff(f(x), x, x) ],
>    x=-2..2, discont=true );
```

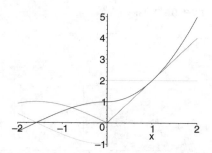

This technique also works for parametrized plots.

```
> plot( [ [ 2*cos(t), sin(t), t=0..2*Pi ],
>            [ t^2, t^3, t=-1..1 ] ], scaling=constrained );
```

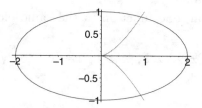

Using different line styles, such as solid, dashed, or dotted, is convenient for distinguishing between several graphs in the same plot. The linestyle option controls this. Use linestyle=SOLID for the first function, $\sin(x)/x$, and linestyle=DOT for the second function, $\cos(x)/x$.

```
> plot( [ sin(x)/x, cos(x)/x ], x=0..8*Pi, y=-0.5..1.5,
> linestyle=[SOLID,DOT] );
```

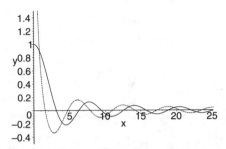

You can also change the line style by using the standard menus and the context-sensitive menus. Similarly, specify the colors of the graphs by using the **color** option. (You can see the effect with a color display but, in this book, the lines appear in two different shades of grey.)

```
> plot( [ [f(x), D(f)(x), x=-2..2],
>          [D(f)(x), (D@@2)(f)(x), x=-2..2] ],
>          color=[gold, plum] );
```

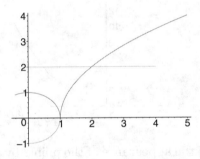

For more details on colors, refer to **?plot,color**.

Plotting Data Points

To plot numeric data, call **pointplot** with the data in a list of lists of the form

$$[[x_1, y_1], [x_2, y_2], \ldots, [x_n, y_n]].$$

If the list is long, assign it to a name.

```
> data_list:=[[-2,4],[-1,1],[0, 0],[1,1],[2,4],[3,9],[4,16]];
```

$$data\_list :=$$
$$[[-2, 4], [-1, 1], [0, 0], [1, 1], [2, 4], [3, 9], [4, 16]]$$

```
> pointplot(data_list);
```

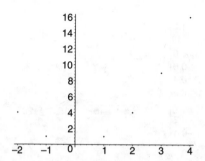

By default, Maple does not join the points with straight lines. Use the **style=line** option to plot the lines. You can also use the menus to draw lines.

```
> pointplot( data_list, style=line );
```

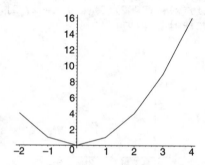

You can change the appearance of the points by using either the menus or the **symbol** and **symbolsize** options.

```
> data_list_2:=[[1,1], [2,2], [3,3], [4,4]];
```

$$data\_list\_2 := [[1, 1], [2, 2], [3, 3], [4, 4]]$$

```
> pointplot(data_list_2, style=point, symbol=cross,
> symbolsize=16);
```

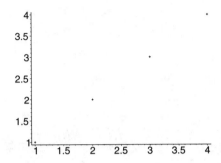

Use the `CurveFitting` package to fit a curve through several points, and then use the `plot` function to see the result. For more information, refer to `?CurveFitting`.

Refining Plots

Maple uses an adaptive plotting algorithm. It calculates the value of the function or expression at a modest number of approximately equidistant points in the specified plotting interval. Maple then computes more points within the subintervals that have large amount of fluctuation. Occasionally, this adaptive algorithm does not produce a satisfactory plot.

```
> plot(sum((-1)^(i)*abs(x-i/10), i=0..50), x=-1..6);
```

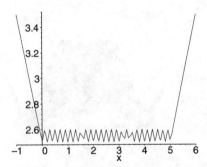

To refine this plot, you can indicate that Maple should compute more points.

```
> plot(sum((-1)^(i)*abs(x-i/10), i=0..50), x=-1..6,
>       numpoints=500);
```

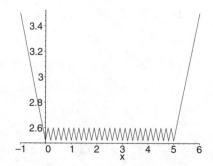

For further details and examples, refer to **?plot** and **?plot,options**.

4.2   Graphing in Three Dimensions

You can plot a function of two variables as a surface in three-dimensional space. This allows you to visualize the function. The syntax for **plot3d** is similar to that for **plot**. Again, an explicit function, $z = f(x, y)$, is easiest to plot.

```
> plot3d( sin(x*y), x=-2..2, y=-2..2 );
```

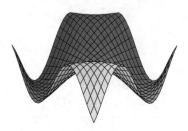

You can rotate the plot by dragging in the plot window. The menus allow you to change various characteristics of a plot.

As with **plot**, **plot3d** can handle user-defined functions.

```
> f := (x,y) -> sin(x) * cos(y);
```

$$f := (x,\ y) \to \sin(x)\cos(y)$$

```
> plot3d( f(x,y), x=0..2*Pi, y=0..2*Pi );
```

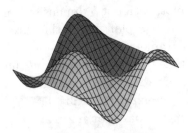

By default, Maple displays the graph as a shaded surface, but you can change this by using either the menus or the **style** option. For example, **style=hidden** draws the graph as a hidden wireframe structure.

```
> plot3d( f(x,y), x=0..2*Pi, y=0..2*Pi, style=hidden );
```

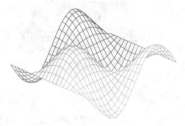

For a list of **style** options, refer to **?plot3d,options**.
The range of the second parameter can depend on the first parameter.

```
> plot3d( sqrt(x-y), x=0..9, y=-x..x );
```

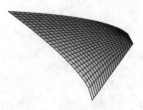

Parametric Plots

You cannot specify some surfaces explicitly as $z = f(x, y)$. The sphere is an example of such a plot. As for two-dimensional graphs (see Section 4.1), one solution is a *parametric* plot. Make the three coordinates, x, y, and z, functions of two parameters, for example, s and t. You can specify parametric plots in three dimensions by using the following syntax.

```
plot3d( [ x-expr, y-expr, z-expr ],
   parameter1=range, parameter2=range )
```

Here are two examples.

```
> plot3d( [ sin(s), cos(s)*sin(t), sin(t) ],
>    s=-Pi..Pi, t=-Pi..Pi );
```

```
> plot3d( [ s*sin(s)*cos(t), s*cos(s)*cos(t), s*sin(t) ],
>    s=0..2*Pi, t=0..Pi );
```

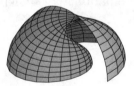

Spherical Coordinates

The Cartesian (ordinary) coordinate system is only one of many coordinate systems in three dimensions. In the spherical coordinate system, the three coordinates are the distance r to the origin, the angle θ in the xy-plane measured in the counterclockwise direction from the x-axis, and the angle ϕ measured from the z-axis.

Figure 4.2 The Spherical Coordinate System

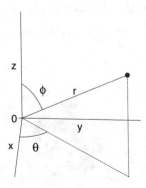

Maple can plot a function in spherical coordinates by using the **sphereplot** command in the **plots** package. To access the command with its short name, use **with(plots)**. To avoid listing all the commands in the **plots** package, use a colon, rather than a semicolon.

```
> with(plots):
```

Use the **sphereplot** command in the following manner.

```
sphereplot( r-expr, theta=range, phi=range )
```

The graph of $r = (4/3)^\theta \sin \phi$ looks like this:

```
> sphereplot( (4/3)^theta * sin(phi),
>    theta=-1..2*Pi, phi=0..Pi );
```

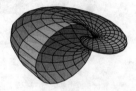

Plotting a sphere in spherical coordinates is easy: specify the radius, perhaps 1, let θ run all the way around the equator, and let ϕ run from the North Pole ($\phi = 0$) to the South Pole ($\phi = \pi$).

```
> sphereplot( 1, theta=0..2*Pi, phi=0..Pi,
>   scaling=constrained );
```

(For more information on constrained versus unconstrained plotting, see section 4.1.)

The **sphereplot** command also accepts parametrized plots, that is, functions that define the radius and both angle-coordinates in terms of two parameters, for example, s and t. The syntax is similar to a parametrized plot in Cartesian (ordinary) coordinates. See this section, page 114.

```
sphereplot( [ r-expr, theta-expr, phi-expr ],
            parameter1=range, parameter2=range )
```

Here $r = \exp(s) + t$, $\theta = \cos(s + t)$, and $\phi = t^2$.

```
> sphereplot( [ exp(s)+t, cos(s+t), t^2 ],
>             s=0..2*Pi, t=-2..2 );
```

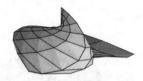

Cylindrical Coordinates

Specify a point in the *cylindrical coordinate system* using the three coordinates r, θ, and z. Here r and θ are polar coordinates (see section 4.1) in the xy-plane and z is the usual Cartesian z-coordinate.

Figure 4.3 The Cylindrical Coordinate System

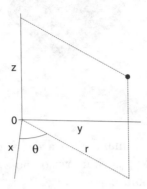

Maple plots functions in cylindrical coordinates with the `cylinderplot` command from the **plots** package.

```
> with(plots):
```

You can plot graphs in cylindrical coordinates by using the following syntax.

```
cylinderplot( r-expr, angle=range, z=range )
```

Here is a three-dimensional version of the spiral previously shown in section 4.1.

```
> cylinderplot( theta, theta=0..4*Pi, z=-1..1 );
```

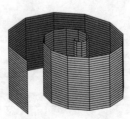

Cones are easy to plot in cylindrical coordinates: let r equal z and let θ vary from 0 to 2π.

```
> cylinderplot( z, theta=0..2*Pi, z=0..1 );
```

The `cylinderplot` command also accepts parametrized plots. The syntax is similar to that of parametrized plots in Cartesian (ordinary) coordinates. See this section, page 114.

```
cylinderplot( [ r-expr, theta-expr, z-expr ],
              parameter1=range, parameter2=range )
```

The following is a plot of $r = st$, $\theta = s$, and $z = \cos(t^2)$.

```
> cylinderplot( [s*t, s, cos(t^2)], s=0..Pi, t=-2..2 );
```

Refining Plots

If your plot is not as smooth or precise as you want, calculate more points. The option for doing this is

```
grid=[m, n]
```

where m is the number of points to use for the first coordinate, and n is the number of points to use for the second coordinate.

```
> plot3d( sin(x)*cos(y), x=0..3*Pi, y=0..3*Pi, grid=[50,50] );
```

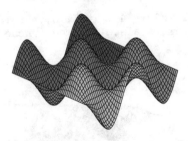

In the next example, a large number of points (100) for the first co-ordinate (`theta`) makes the spiral look smooth. However, the function does not change in the `z`-direction. Thus, a small number of points (5) is sufficient.

```
> cylinderplot( theta, theta=0..4*Pi, z=-1..1, grid=[100,5] );
```

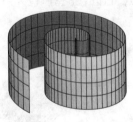

The default `grid` is approximately 25 by 25 points.

Shading and Lighting Schemes

Two methods for shading a surface in a three-dimensional plot are available. In the first method, one or more distinctly colored light sources illuminate the surface. In the second method, the color of each point is a direct function of its coordinates.

Maple has a number of preselected light source configurations which give aesthetically pleasing results. You can choose from these light sources through the menus or with the `lightmodel` option. For coloring the surface directly, a number of predefined coloring functions are also available through the menus or with the `shading` option.

Simultaneous use of light sources and direct coloring may complicate the resulting coloring. Use either light sources *or* direct coloring. Here is a surface colored with `zgrayscale shading` and no lighting.

```
> plot3d( x*y^2/(x^2+y^4), x=-5..5,y=-5..5,
>     shading=zgrayscale, lightmodel=none );
```

The same surface illuminated by lighting scheme `light1` and no **shading** follows.

```
> plot3d( x*y^2/(x^2+y^4), x=-5..5,y=-5..5,
>     shading=none, lightmodel=light1 );
```

The plots appear in black and white in this book. Try them in Maple to see the effects in color.

4.3   Animation

Graphing is an excellent way to represent information. However, static plots do not always emphasize certain graphical behavior, such as the deformation of a bouncing ball, as effectively as their animated counterparts.

A Maple animation is a number of plot frames displayed in sequence, similar to the action of movie frames. The two commands used for animations, `animate` and `animate3d`, are defined in the `plots` package. Remember that to access the commands using the short name, use the `with(plots)` command.

Animation in Two Dimensions

You can specify a two-dimensional animation by using this syntax.

```
animate( y-expr, x=range, time=range )
```

The following is an example of an animation.

```
> with(plots):
```

```
Warning, the name changecoords has been redefined
```

```
> animate( sin(x*t), x=-10..10, t=1..2 );
```

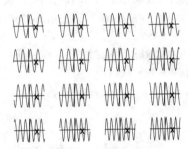

To play an animation you must first select it by clicking it. Then choose **Play** from the **Animation** menu.

By default, a two-dimensional animation consists of sixteen plots (`frames`). If the motion is not smooth, you can increase the number of frames. Please note that computing many frames may require a lot of time and memory. The following command can be pasted into Maple to produce an animation with 50 frames.

```
> animate( sin(x*t), x=-10..10, t=1..2, frames=50);
```

The usual `plot` options are also available. Enter the following example into Maple to view the animation.

```
> animate( sin(x*t), x=-10..10, t=1..2,
>    frames=50, numpoints=100 );
```

You can plot any two-dimensional animation as a three-dimensional static plot. For example, try plotting the animation of $\sin(xt)$ above as a surface.

```
> plot3d( sin(x*t), x=-10..10, t=1..2, grid=[50,100],
>    orientation=[135,45], axes=boxed , style=HIDDEN );
```

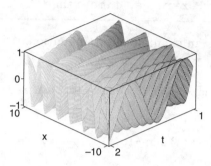

Whether you prefer an animation or a plot is a matter of taste and also depends on the concepts that the animation or plot is supposed to convey.

Animating parametrized graphs is also possible. For more information on parametrized graphes, see section 4.1.

```
> animate( [ a*cos(u), sin(u), u=0..2*Pi ], a=0..2 );
```

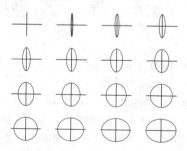

By using the **coords** option, **animate** uses a coordinate system other than the Cartesian (ordinary) system.

```
> animate( theta*t, theta=0..8*Pi, t=1..4, coords=polar );
```

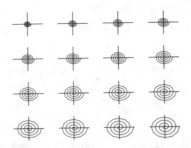

To view the actual animations, enter the commands for the animations in Maple.

Animation in Three Dimensions

Use `animate3d` to animate surfaces in three dimensions. You can use the `animate3d` command as follows.

```
animate3d( z-expr, x=range, y=range, time=range )
```

The following is an example of a three-dimensional animation.

```
> animate3d( cos(t*x)*sin(t*y),
>            x=-Pi..Pi, y=-Pi..Pi, t=1..2 );
```

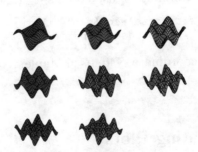

By default, a three-dimensional animation consists of eight plots. As for two-dimensional animations, the `frames` option determines the number of frames.

```
> animate3d( cos(t*x)*sin(t*y), x=-Pi..Pi, y=-Pi..Pi, t=1..2,
>     frames=16 );
```

Section 4.2 describes three-dimensional parametrized plots. You can also animate these.

```
> animate3d( [s*time, t-time, s*cos(t*time)],
>     s=1..3, t=1..4, time=2..4, axes=boxed);
```

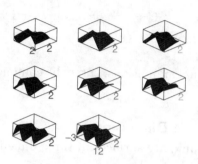

To animate a function in a coordinate system other than the Cartesian, use the **coords** option. Enter the following examples into Maple to view the animations. For spherical coordinates, use **coords=spherical**.

```
> animate3d( (1.3)^theta * sin(t*phi), theta=-1..2*Pi,
>     phi=0..Pi, t=1..8, coords=spherical );
```

For cylindrical coordinates, use **coords=cylindrical**.

```
> animate3d( sin(theta)*cos(z*t), theta=1..3, z=1..4,
>     t=1/4..7/2, coords=cylindrical );
```

For a list of the coordinate systems in Maple, refer to **?plots,changecoords**.

4.4   Annotating Plots

Adding text annotation to plots is possible in a variety of ways. The option **title** prints the specified title in the plot window, centered and near the top.

```
> plot( sin(x), x=-2*Pi..2*Pi, title="Plot of Sine" );
```

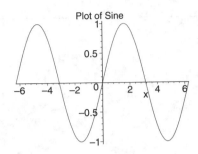

Note that when specifying the title you must place double quotes (")
at both ends of the text. This is very important. Maple uses double quotes
to delimit strings. It considers whatever appears between double quotes
to be a piece of text that it should not process further. You can specify
the font, style, and size of the title with the `titlefont` option.

```
> with(plots):
```

Warning, the name changecoords has been redefined

```
> sphereplot( 1, theta=0..2*Pi, phi=0..Pi,
>     scaling=constrained, title="The Sphere",
>     titlefont=[HELVETICA, BOLD, 24] );
```

The Sphere

The `labels` option enables you to specify the labels on the axes, the
`labelsfont` option gives you control over the font and style of the labels,
and the `labeldirections` option enables you to place axis labels either
vertically or horizontally. Note that the labels do not have to match the
variables in the expression you are plotting.

```
> plot( x^2, x=0..3, labels=["time", "velocity"],
>          labeldirections=[horizontal,vertical] );
```

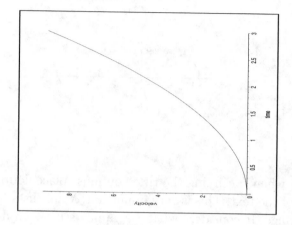

You can print labels only if your plot displays axes. For three-dimensional graphs, there are no axes by default. You must use the **axes** option.

```
> plot3d( sin(x*y), x=-1..1, y=-1..1,
>     labels=["length", "width", "height"], axes=FRAMED );
```

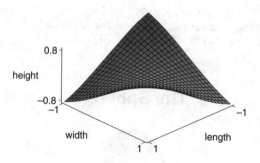

The **legend** option enables you to add a text legend to your plot.

```
> plot( [sin(x), cos(x)], x=-3*Pi/2..3*Pi/2, linestyle=[1,4],
>       legend=["The Sine Function", "The Cosine Function"] );
```

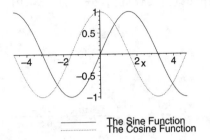

The Sine Function
The Cosine Function

4.5   Composite Plots

Maple allows you to display several plots simultaneously, after assigning names to the individual plots. Since plot structures are usually rather large, end the assignments with colons (rather than semicolons).

```
> my_plot := plot( sin(x), x=-10..10 ):
```
Now you can save the plot for future use, as you would any other expression. Exhibit the plot by using the **display** command defined in the **plots** package.

```
> with(plots):
```

```
> display( my_plot );
```

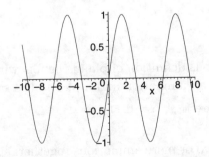

The **display** command can draw several plots at the same time. Simply give a list of plots.

```
> a := plot( [ sin(t), exp(t)/20, t=-Pi..Pi ] ):
> b := polarplot( [ sin(t), exp(t), t=-Pi..Pi ] ):
> display( [a,b] );
```

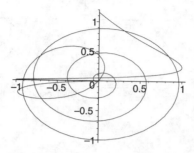

This technique allows you to display plots of different types in the same axes. You can also display three-dimensional plots, even animations.

```
> c := sphereplot( 1, theta=0..2*Pi, phi=0..Pi ):
```

```
> d := cylinderplot( 0.5, theta=0..2*Pi, z=-2..2 ):
> display( [c,d], scaling=constrained );
```

Enter the previous definition of b and the following Maple commands into Maple to view an animation and a plot in the same axes.

```
> e := animate( m*x, x=-1..1, m=-1..1 ):
> display( [b,e] );
```

If you display two or more animations together, ensure that they have the same number of frames. Enter the following example into Maple to view two animations simultaneously.

```
> f := animate3d( sin(x+y+t), x=0..2*Pi, y=0..2*Pi, t=0..5,
>       frames=20 ):
> g := animate3d( t, x=0..2*Pi, y=0..2*Pi, t=-1.5..1.5,
>       frames=20):
> display( [f,g] );
```

Placing Text in Plots

The `title` and `labels` options to the plotting commands allow you to put titles and labels on your graphs. The `textplot` and `textplot3d` commands give more flexibility by allowing you to specify the exact positions of the text. The `plots` package contains these two commands.

```
> with(plots):
```

You can use `textplot` and `textplot3d` as follows.

```
textplot( [ x-coord, y-coord, "text" ] );
textplot3d( [ x-coord, y-coord, z-coord, "text"] );
```

For example,

```
> a := plot( sin(x), x=-Pi..Pi ):
> b := textplot( [ Pi/2, 1, "Local Maximum" ] ):
> c := textplot( [ -Pi/2, -1, "Local Minimum" ] ):
> display( [a,b,c] );
```

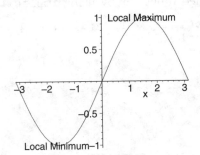

For details on controlling the placement of text, refer to `?plots,textplot`. Use the `font` option to specify the font `textplot` and `textplot3d` use. In the following plot, the origin, a saddle point, is labelled P.

```
> d := plot3d( x^2-y^2, x=-1..1, y=-1..1 ):
> e := textplot3d( [0, 0, 0, "P"],
>       font=[HELVETICA, OBLIQUE, 22], color=white ):
> display( [d,e], orientation=[68,45] );
```

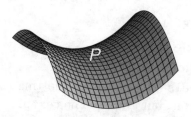

4.6   Special Types of Plots

The plots package contains many routines for producing special types of graphics.

Here is a variety of examples. For further explanation of a particular plot command, refer to ?plots,command.

```
> with(plots):
```

Plot implicitly defined functions by using implicitplot.

```
> implicitplot( x^2+y^2=1, x=-1..1, y=-1..1, scaling=
>    constrained );
```

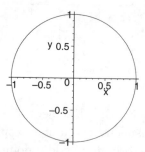

Below is a plot of the region satisfying the inequalities $x + y < 5$, $0 < x$, and $x \leq 4$.

```
> inequal( {x+y<5, 0<x, x<=4}, x=-1..5, y=-10..10,
>     optionsexcluded=(color=yellow) );
```

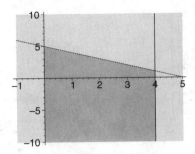

Here the vertical axis has a logarithmic scale.

```
> logplot( 10^x, x=0..10 );
```

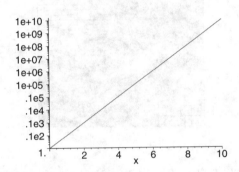

A `semilogplot` has a logarithmic horizontal axis.

```
> semilogplot( 2^(sin(x)), x=1..10 );
```

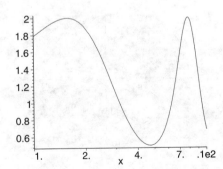

Maple can also create plots where both axes have logarithmic scales.

```
> loglogplot( x^17, x=1..7 );
```

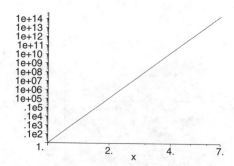

In a **densityplot**, lighter shading indicates a larger function value.

```
> densityplot( sin(x*y), x=-1..1, y=-1..1 );
```

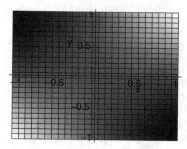

Along the following curves, $\sin(xy)$ is constant, as in a topographical map.

```
> contourplot(sin(x*y),x=-10..10,y=-10..10);
```

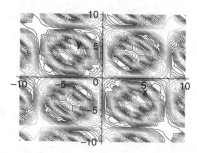

A rectangular grid in the complex plane becomes the following graph when you map it by $z \mapsto z^2$.

```
> conformal( z^2, z=0..2+2*I );
```

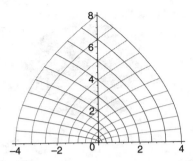

The `fieldplot` command draws the given vector for many values of x and y. That is, it plots a vector field, such as a magnetic field.

```
> fieldplot( [y*cos(x*y), x*cos(x*y)], x=-1..1, y=-1..1);
```

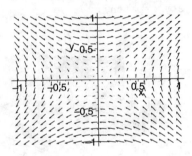

Maple can draw curves in three-dimensional space.

```
> spacecurve( [cos(t),sin(t),t], t=0..12 );
```

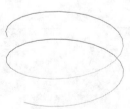

Here Maple inflates the previous spacecurve to form a tube.

```
> tubeplot( [cos(t),sin(t),t], t=0..4*Pi, radius=0.5 );
```

The `matrixplot` command plots the values of a object of type Matrix.

```
> A := LinearAlgebra[HilbertMatrix](8):
> B := LinearAlgebra[ToeplitzMatrix]([1,2,3,4,-4,-3,-2,-1],
>     symmetric):
> matrixplot( A+B, heights=histogram, axes=frame,
>     gap=0.25, style=patch);
```

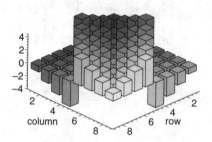

The following is a demonstration of a root locus plot.

```
> rootlocus( (s^5-1)/(s^2+1), s, -5..5, style=point,
>     adaptive=false );
```

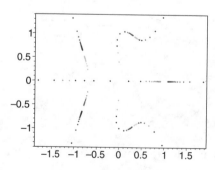

The `arrow` command plots arrows or vectors in two or three dimensions.

```
> plots[arrow]( [<2, 1>, <3, 2>], [<2, 5>, <1, 4>], difference,
>    scaling=constrained );
```

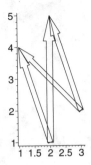

For a listing of other available plot types, enter `?plots` at the Maple prompt.

4.7   Manipulating Graphical Objects

The `plottools` package contains commands for creating graphical objects and manipulating their plots. Use `with(plottools)` to access the commands using the short names.

```
> with(plottools):
```

The objects in the `plottools` package do not automatically display. You must use the `display` command, defined in the `plots` package.

```
> with(plots):
```

Consider the following example.

```
> display( dodecahedron(), scaling=constrained, style=patch );
```

Give an object a name.

```
> s1 := sphere( [3/2,1/4,1/2], 1/4, color=red):
```

Note that the assignment ends with a colon (:). If you use a semicolon
(;), Maple displays a large plot structure. Again, you must use **display**
to see the plot.

```
> display( s1, scaling=constrained );
```

Place a second sphere in the picture and display the axes.

```
> s2 := sphere( [3/2,-1/4,1/2], 1/4, color=red):
> display( [s1, s2], axes=normal, scaling=constrained );
```

Color Plates

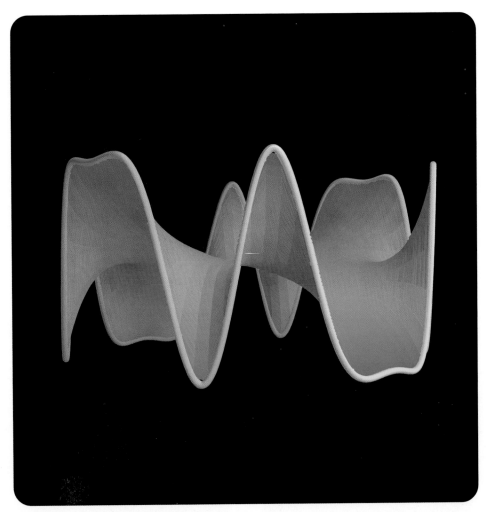

Plate 1: Dirichlet Problem for a Circle

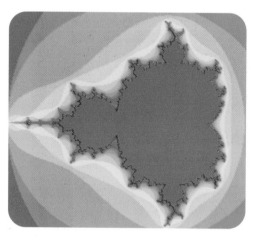

Plate 2: Mandelbrot Set

Plate 3: Origami Bird

Plate 4: Conchoid

Plate 5: Gauss Map
Graphed on a Torus

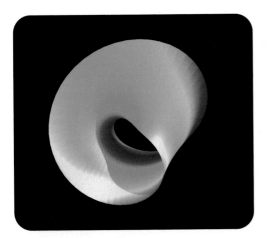

Plate 6: Moebius Strip

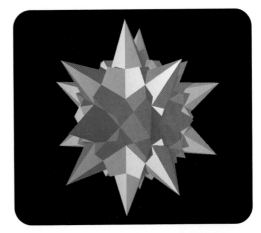

Plate 7: Icosahedron

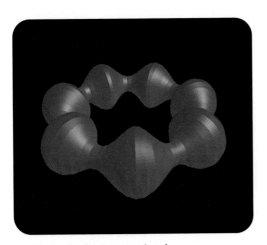

Plate 8: Parameterized
Surface of Revolution

Plate 9: Snowmen

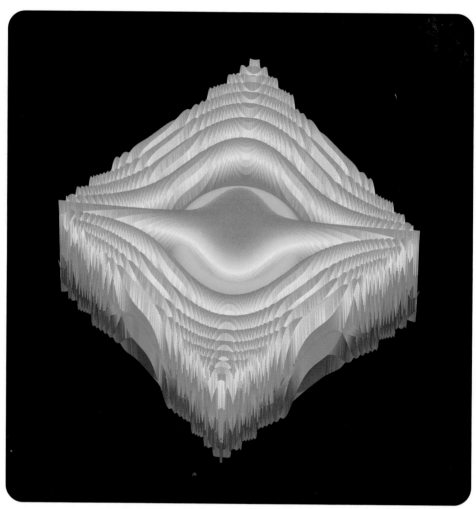

Plate 10: Function of Two Variables in Cartesian Coordinates

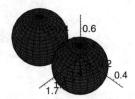

You can also make cones with the `plottools` package.

```
> c := cone([0,0,0], 1/2, 2, color=khaki):
> display( c, axes=normal );
```

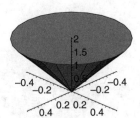

Experiment using Maple's object rotation capabilities.

```
> c2 := rotate( c, 0, Pi/2, 0 ):
> display( c2, axes=normal );
```

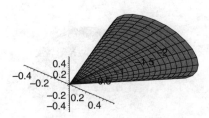

You can also translate objects. .

```
> c3 := translate( c2, 3, 0, 1/4 ):
> display( c3, axes=normal );
```

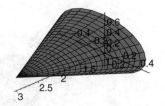

The **hemisphere** command makes a hemisphere. You can specify the radius and the coordinates of the center. Otherwise, leave an empty set of parentheses to accept the defaults.

```
> cup := hemisphere():
> display( cup );
```

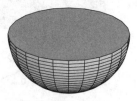

```
> cap := rotate( cup, Pi, 0, 0 ):
> display( cap );
```

All the sides of the dodecahedron mentioned earlier in this section are pentagons. If you raise the midpoint of each pentagon by using the `stellate` command, the term for the resulting object is *stellated* dodecahedron.

```
> a := stellate( dodecahedron() ):
> display( a, scaling=constrained, style=patch );
```

```
> stelhs := stellate(cap, 2):
> display( stelhs );
```

Instead of stellating the dodecahedron, you can cut out, for example, the inner three quarters of each pentagon.

```
> a := cutout( dodecahedron(), 3/4 ):
> display( a, scaling=constrained, orientation=[45, 30] );
```

```
> hedgehog := [s1, s2, c3, stelhs]:
> display( hedgehog, scaling=constrained,
>    style=patchnogrid );
```

4.8   Code for Color Plates

Generating impressive graphics in Maple may require only a few lines of code as shown by the examples in this section. However, other graphics require many lines of code. Code for the color plates[1] that do not have code included can be found in the Maple Application Center.

There are two ways to access the Maple Application Center.

- Open your Internet browser of choice and enter http://www.mapleapps.com

- From the **Help** menu in your Maple 8 session, select **Maple on the Web**, and **Application Center**.

To access color plate code not included:

1. Go to the Maple Application Center.

2. Scroll to the bottom of the page. In the **Maple Tools** section, click **Maple 8 Color Plates**. The code is available in both HTML and Maple Worksheet formats.

Hundreds of graphics, including animations, are also available in the Maple Graphics Gallery and in the Maple Animation Gallery. To access these galleries, go to the Maple Application Center and click **Maple Graphics**.

---

[1]Several of the color plates provided were exported and rendered in POV-Ray^{TM}. As a result, exact duplication of these images may be difficult.

Note: On some computers, the `numpoints` options value may need to be decreased to generate the plot.

1. **Dirichlet Problem for a Circle**

```
> with(plots):
> setoptions3d(scaling=constrained, projection=0.5,
> style=patchnogrid):
> f1 := (x, y) -> 0.5*sin(10*x*y):
> f2 := t -> f1(cos(t), sin(t)):
> a0 := evalf(Int(f2(t), t=-Pi..Pi)/Pi):
> a := seq(evalf(Int(f2(t)*cos(n*t), t=-Pi..Pi)/Pi), n=1..50):
> b := seq(evalf(Int(f2(t)*sin(n*t), t=-Pi..Pi)/Pi), n=1..50):
> L := (r, s) -> a0/2+sum('r^n*(a[n]*cos(n*s)+b[n]*sin(n*s))',
> 'n'=1..50):
> q := plot3d([r*cos(s), r*sin(s), L(r, s)], r=0..1, s=0..2*Pi,
> color=[L(r, s), -L(r, s), 0.2], grid=[29, 100],
> numpoints=10000):
> p := tubeplot([cos(t), sin(t), f2(t), t=-Pi..Pi,
> radius=0.015], tubepoints=70, numpoints=1500):
> display3d({q, p}, orientation=[3, 89], lightmodel=light2);
```

2. **Mandelbrot Set**

The Mandelbrot Set is one of the most complex objects in mathematics given the chaotic nature that surrounds the image. Code for this graphic is available at the Maple Application Center.

3. **Origami Bird**

The Origami Bird can be displayed as a simple graphic as well as a Maple animation. Code for the graphic and the animation are available at the Maple Application Center.

4. **Conchoid**

Code for this and other seashells is available at the Maple Application Center.

5. **Gauss Map Graphed on a Torus**

```
> sp := [rho*cos(2*Pi*t), rho*sin(2*Pi*t), 0, radius=b]:
> pc := n -> [ (rho-r*cos(2*Pi*t))*cos(2*Pi/(n+t)),
>            (rho-r*cos(2*Pi*t))*sin(2*Pi/(n+t)),
>            -r*sin(2*Pi*t)]:
> rho, r, b := 3, 1.1, 1:
> with(plots):
> s := spacecurve( {seq(pc(k),  k=1..50)}, t=0..1, thickness=2,
> color=blue, view=[-4.4..4.4, -4.4..4.4, -2.2..2.2]):
> s2 := tubeplot( sp, t=0..1, tubepoints=20, color=green,
> view=[-4.4..4.4, -4.4..4.4, -2.2..2.2], style=PATCHNOGRID,
> lightmodel=light2 ):
```

```
> display( {s,s2} );
```

6. Moebius Strip

```
> moebius := plot3d([4+x*cos(1/2*y), y, x*sin(1/2*y)],
> x=-Pi..Pi, y=-0..2*Pi, coords=cylindrical, style=patchnogrid,
> grid=[60,60], orientation=[-176, 45], lightmodel=light3,
> shading=zhue, scaling=constrained):
> plots[display](moebius);
```

7. Icosahedron

```
> with(geom3d):
> icosahedron(p1, point(o, 0, 0, 0), 1):
> stellate(p2, p1, 4):
> p := draw(p2):
> q := plottools[homothety](p,3):
> plots[display]([p,q], scaling=constrained, style=patchnogrid,
> lightmodel=light4, shading=xyz, orientation=[-107,81]);
```

To view other variations, change the height value in the stellate command.

8. Parameterized Surface of Revolution

```
> r1 := 2 + sin(7*t):
> z1 := r1*cos(s):
> r2 := 8+r1*sin(s):
> plot3d([r2*sin(t), r2*cos(t), z1], s=0..2*Pi, t=0..2*Pi,
> grid=[80, 80], axes=none, style=patchnogrid, lightmodel=light1);
```

9. Snowmen

The Snowmen graphic is an animation. Code for this animation is available at the Maple Application Center.

10. Function of Two Variables in Cartesian Coordinates

```
> plot3d({sin(x^2+y^2), 2*cos(x^3+y^3)}, x=-3..3, y=-3..3,
> style=patch, grid=[120, 120], axes=none, shading=zhue,
> style=patchnogrid, scaling=constrained, orientation=[50,30]);
```

4.9 Conclusion

This chapter examined Maple's two- and three-dimensional plotting capabilities, involving explicitly, parametrically, and implicitly given functions. Cartesian, polar, spherical, and cylindrical are a few of the many coordinate systems that Maple can handle. Furthermore, you can animate a graph and shade it in a variety of ways for a clearer understanding of its nature.

Use the commands found in the `plots` package to display various graphs of functions and expressions. Some of the special plot types that you can create using these commands include contour, density, and logarithmic plots. The commands within the `plottools` package create and manipulate objects. Such commands, for instance, allow you to translate, rotate, and even stellate a graphical entity.

5 Evaluation and Simplification

In Maple, a significant amount of time and effort is spent manipulating expressions. Expression manipulation is done for many reasons, from converting output expressions into a familiar form to check answers, to converting expressions into a specific form needed by certain Maple routines.

The issue of simplification is surprisingly difficult in symbolic mathematics. What is simple in one context may not be in another context—each individual context can have its own definition of a "simple" form.

Maple provides a set of tools for working with expressions, for performing both mathematical and structural manipulations. Mathematical manipulations are those that correspond to some kind of standard mathematical process, for example, factoring a polynomial, or rationalizing the denominator of a rational expression. Structural manipulation tools allow you to access and modify parts of the Maple data structures that represent expressions and other types of objects.

5.1   Mathematical Manipulations

Solving equations by hand usually involves performing a sequence of algebraic manipulations. You can also perform these steps using Maple.

```
> eq := 4*x + 17 = 23;
```

$$eq := 4\,x + 17 = 23$$

Here, you must subtract 17 from both sides of the equation. To do so, subtract the equation 17=17 from **eq**. Make sure to put parentheses around the unnamed equation.

```
> eq - ( 17 = 17 );
```

$$4\,x = 6$$

Now divide through by 4. Note that you do not have to use 4=4 in this case.

```
> % / 4;
```

$$x = \frac{3}{2}$$

The following sections focus on more sophisticated manipulations.

Expanding Polynomials as Sums

Sums are generally easier to comprehend than products, so you may find it useful to expand a polynomial as a sum of products. The **expand** command has this capability.

```
> poly := (x+1)*(x+2)*(x+5)*(x-3/2);
```

$$poly := (x + 1)\,(x + 2)\,(x + 5)\left(x - \frac{3}{2}\right)$$

```
> expand( poly );
```

$$x^4 + \frac{13}{2}\,x^3 + 5\,x^2 - \frac{31}{2}\,x - 15$$

The **expand** command expands the numerator of a rational expression.

```
> expand( (x+1)*(y^2-2*y+1) / z / (y-1) );
```

$$\frac{x\,y^2}{z\,(y - 1)} - 2\,\frac{x\,y}{z\,(y - 1)} + \frac{x}{z\,(y - 1)} + \frac{y^2}{z\,(y - 1)} - 2\,\frac{y}{z\,(y - 1)}$$
$$+ \frac{1}{z\,(y - 1)}$$

Use the `normal` command to cancel common factors. See this section, page 155.

The `expand` command also recognizes expansion rules for many standard mathematical functions.

```
> expand( sin(2*x) );
```

$$2\sin(x)\cos(x)$$

```
> ln( abs(x^2)/(1+abs(x)) );
```

$$\ln(\frac{|x|^2}{1+|x|})$$

```
> expand(%);
```

$$2\ln(|x|) - \ln(1+|x|)$$

The `combine` command knows the same rules but applies them in the opposite direction. For information on combining terms, see this section, page 154.

You can specify subexpressions that you do *not* want to expand, as an argument to `expand`.

```
> expand( (x+1)*(y+z) );
```

$$x\,y + x\,z + y + z$$

```
> expand( (x+1)*(y+z), x+1 );
```

$$(x+1)\,y + (x+1)\,z$$

You can expand an expression over a special domain.

```
> poly := (x+2)^2*(x-2)*(x+3)*(x-1)^2*(x-1);
```

$$poly := (x+2)^2\,(x-2)\,(x+3)\,(x-1)^3$$

```
> expand( poly );
```

$$x^7 + 2\,x^6 - 10\,x^5 - 12\,x^4 + 37\,x^3 + 10\,x^2 - 52\,x + 24$$

```
> % mod 3;
```

$$x^7 + 2\,x^6 + 2\,x^5 + x^3 + x^2 + 2\,x$$

However, using the **Expand** command is more efficient.

```
> Expand( poly ) mod 3;
```

$$x^7 + 2\,x^6 + 2\,x^5 + x^3 + x^2 + 2\,x$$

When you use **Expand** with **mod**, Maple performs all intermediate calculations in modulo arithmetic. You can also write your own **expand** subroutines. For more details, refer to **?expand**.

Collecting the Coefficients of Like Powers

An expression like $x^2 + 2x + 1 - ax + b - cx^2$ may be easier to read if you collect the coefficients of x^2, x, and the constant terms, by using the **collect** command.

```
> collect( x^2 + 2*x + 1 - a*x + b - c*x^2, x );
```

$$(1 - c)\,x^2 + (2 - a)\,x + b + 1$$

The second argument to the **collect** command specifies on which variable it should base the collection.

```
> poly := x^2 + 2*y*x - 3*y + y^2*x^2;
```

$$poly := x^2 + 2\,y\,x - 3\,y + y^2\,x^2$$

```
> collect( poly, x );
```

$$(1 + y^2)\,x^2 + 2\,y\,x - 3\,y$$

```
> collect( poly, y );
```

$$y^2\,x^2 + (2\,x - 3)\,y + x^2$$

You can collect on either variables or unevaluated function calls.

```
> trig_expr := sin(x)*cos(x) + sin(x) + y*sin(x);
```

$$trig\_expr := \sin(x)\cos(x) + \sin(x) + y\sin(x)$$

```
> collect( trig_expr, sin(x) );
```

$$(\cos(x) + 1 + y)\sin(x)$$

```
> DE := diff(f(x),x,x)*sin(x) - diff(f(x),x)*sin(f(x))
>     + sin(x)*diff(f(x),x) + sin(f(x))*diff(f(x),x,x);
```

$$DE := (\tfrac{d^2}{dx^2}\,f(x))\sin(x) - (\tfrac{d}{dx}\,f(x))\sin(f(x)) + \sin(x)\,(\tfrac{d}{dx}\,f(x))$$
$$+ \sin(f(x))\,(\tfrac{d^2}{dx^2}\,f(x))$$

```
> collect( DE, diff );
```

$$(-\sin(f(x)) + \sin(x))\,(\frac{d}{dx}\,f(x)) + (\sin(x) + \sin(f(x)))\,(\frac{d^2}{dx^2}\,f(x))$$

You cannot collect on sums or products.

```
> big_expr := z*x*y + 2*x*y + z;
```

$$big\_expr := z\,x\,y + 2\,y\,x + z$$

```
> collect( big_expr, x*y );
```

```
Error, (in collect) cannot collect y*x
```

Instead, make a substitution before you collect. In the preceding case, substituting a dummy name for x*y, then collecting on the dummy name produces the desired result.

```
> subs( x=xyprod/y, big_expr );
```

$$z\,xyprod + 2\,xyprod + z$$

```
> collect( %, xyprod );
```

$$(z + 2)\,xyprod + z$$

```
> subs( xyprod=x*y, % );
```

$$(z+2)\,y\,x + z$$

Section 5.3 explains the use of the subs command.

If you are collecting coefficients of more than one variable simultaneously, two options are available, the recursive and distributed forms. Recursive form initially collects in the first specified variable, then in the next, and so on. The default is the recursive form.

```
> poly := x*y + z*x*y + y*x^2 - z*y*x^2 + x + z*x;
```

$$poly := y\,x + z\,x\,y + y\,x^2 - z\,y\,x^2 + x + z\,x$$

```
> collect( poly, [x,y] );
```

$$(1-z)\,y\,x^2 + ((1+z)\,y + 1 + z)\,x$$

Distributed form collects the coefficients of all variables at the same time.

```
> collect( poly, [x,y], distributed );
```

$$(1+z)\,x + (1+z)\,y\,x + (1-z)\,y\,x^2$$

The collect command does not sort the terms. Use the sort command to sort. See this section, page 160.

Factoring Polynomials and Rational Functions

You may want to write a polynomial as a product of terms of smallest possible degree. Use the factor command to factor polynomials.

```
> factor( x^2-1 );
```

$$(x-1)\,(x+1)$$

```
> factor( x^3+y^3 );
```

$$(x+y)\,(x^2 - y\,x + y^2)$$

You can also factor rational functions. The factor command factors both the numerator and the denominator, then removes common terms.

```
> rat_expr := (x^16 - y^16) / (x^8 - y^8);
```

$$rat\_expr := \frac{x^{16} - y^{16}}{x^8 - y^8}$$

```
> factor( rat_expr );
```

$$x^8 + y^8$$

```
> rat_expr := (x^16 - y^16) / (x^7 - y^7);
```

$$rat\_expr := \frac{x^{16} - y^{16}}{x^7 - y^7}$$

```
> factor(rat_expr);
```

$$\frac{(y + x)(x^2 + y^2)(x^4 + y^4)(x^8 + y^8)}{x^6 + y\,x^5 + y^2\,x^4 + y^3\,x^3 + y^4\,x^2 + y^5\,x + y^6}$$

Specifying the Algebraic Number Field   The `factor` command factors a polynomial over the ring implied by the coefficients. The following polynomial has integer coefficients, so the terms in the factored form have integer coefficients.

```
> poly := x^5 - x^4 - x^3 + x^2 - 2*x + 2;
```

$$poly := x^5 - x^4 - x^3 + x^2 - 2\,x + 2$$

```
> factor( poly );
```

$$(x - 1)(x^2 - 2)(x^2 + 1)$$

In this next example, the coefficients include $\sqrt{2}$. Note the differences in the result.

```
> expand( sqrt(2)*poly );
```

$$\sqrt{2}\,x^5 - \sqrt{2}\,x^4 - \sqrt{2}\,x^3 + \sqrt{2}\,x^2 - 2\,\sqrt{2}\,x + 2\,\sqrt{2}$$

```
> factor( % );
```

$$\sqrt{2}\,(x^2+1)\,(x+\sqrt{2})\,(x-\sqrt{2})\,(x-1)$$

You can explicitly extend the coefficient field by giving a second argument to `factor`.

```
> poly := x^4 - 5*x^2 + 6;
```

$$poly := x^4 - 5\,x^2 + 6$$

```
> factor( poly );
```

$$(x^2-2)\,(x^2-3)$$

```
> factor( poly, sqrt(2) );
```

$$(x^2-3)\,(x+\sqrt{2})\,(x-\sqrt{2})$$

```
> factor( poly, { sqrt(2), sqrt(3) } );
```

$$-(x+\sqrt{2})\,(x-\sqrt{2})\,(-x+\sqrt{3})\,(x+\sqrt{3})$$

You can also specify the extension by using `RootOf`. Here `RootOf(x^2-2)` represents any solution to $x^2 - 2 = 0$, that is either $\sqrt{2}$ or $-\sqrt{2}$.

```
> factor( poly, RootOf(x^2-2) );
```

$$(x^2-3)\,(x+\mathrm{RootOf}(\_Z^2-2))\,(x-\mathrm{RootOf}(\_Z^2-2))$$

For more information on performing calculations in an algebraic number field, refer to `?evala`.

Factoring in Special Domains Use the `Factor` command to factor an expression over the integers modulo p for some prime p. The syntax is similar to that of the `Expand` command.

```
> Factor( x^2+3*x+3 ) mod 7;
```

$$(x+4)\,(x+6)$$

The `Factor` command also allows algebraic field extensions.

```
> Factor( x^3+1 ) mod 5;
```

$$(x^2 + 4x + 1)(x + 1)$$

```
> Factor( x^3+1, RootOf(x^2+x+1) ) mod 5;
```

$$(x + 4\operatorname{RootOf}(\_Z^2 + \_Z + 1) + 4)(x + 1)$$
$$(x + \operatorname{RootOf}(\_Z^2 + \_Z + 1))$$

For details about the algorithm used, factoring multivariate polynomials, or factoring polynomials over an algebraic number field, refer to ?Factor.

Removing Rational Exponents

In general, it is preferred to represent rational expressions without fractional exponents in the denominator. The **rationalize** command removes roots from the denominator of a rational expression by multiplying by a suitable factor.

```
> 1 / ( 2 + root[3](2) );
```

$$\frac{1}{2 + 2^{(1/3)}}$$

```
> rationalize( % );
```

$$\frac{2}{5} - \frac{1}{5} 2^{(1/3)} + \frac{1}{10} 2^{(2/3)}$$

```
> (x^2+5) / (x + x^(5/7));
```

$$\frac{x^2 + 5}{x + x^{(5/7)}}$$

```
> rationalize( % );
```

$$(x^2 + 5)(x^{(6/7)} - x^{(12/7)} - x^{(4/7)} + x^{(10/7)} + x^{(2/7)} - x^{(8/7)} + x^2)$$
$$/(x^3 + x)$$

The result of **rationalize** is often larger than the original.

Combining Terms

The `combine` command applies a number of transformation rules for various mathematical functions.

```
> combine( sin(x)^2 + cos(x)^2 );
```

$$1$$

```
> combine( sin(x)*cos(x) );
```

$$\frac{1}{2}\sin(2\,x)$$

```
> combine( exp(x)^2 * exp(y) );
```

$$e^{(2\,x+y)}$$

```
> combine( (x^a)^2 );
```

$$x^{(2\,a)}$$

To see how `combine` arrives at the result, give `infolevel[combine]` a positive value.

```
> infolevel[combine] := 1;
```

$$infolevel_{combine} := 1$$

```
> expr := Int(1, x) + Int(x^2, x);
```

$$expr := \int 1\,dx + \int x^2\,dx$$

```
> combine( expr );
combine:    combining with respect to    Int
combine:    combining with respect to    linear
combine:    combining with respect to    int
combine:    combining with respect to    linear
combine:    combining with respect to    Int
combine:    combining with respect to    linear
combine:    combining with respect to    int
combine:    combining with respect to    linear
combine:    combining with respect to    Int
combine:    combining with respect to    linear
```

```
combine:   combining with respect to   cmbplus
combine:   combining with respect to   cmbpwr
combine:   combining with respect to   power
```

$$\int x^2 + 1 \, dx$$

The **expand** command applies most of these transformation rules in the other direction. See this section, page 146.

Factored Normal Form

If an expression contains fractions, you may find it useful to turn the expression into one large fraction, and cancel common factors in the numerator and denominator. The **normal** command performs this process, which often leads to simpler expressions.

```
> normal( x + 1/x );
```

$$\frac{x^2 + 1}{x}$$

```
> expr := x/(x+1) + 1/x + 1/(1+x);
```

$$expr := \frac{x}{x+1} + \frac{1}{x} + \frac{1}{x+1}$$

```
> normal( expr );
```

$$\frac{x+1}{x}$$

```
> expr := (x^2 - y^2) / (x-y)^3;
```

$$expr := \frac{x^2 - y^2}{(x-y)^3}$$

```
> normal( expr );
```

$$\frac{x+y}{(x-y)^2}$$

```
> expr := (x - 1/x) / (x-2);
```

$$expr := \frac{x - \dfrac{1}{x}}{x - 2}$$

```
> normal( expr );
```

$$\frac{x^2 - 1}{x\,(x - 2)}$$

Use the second argument **expanded** if you want **normal** to expand the numerator and the denominator.

```
> normal( expr, expanded );
```

$$\frac{x^2 - 1}{x^2 - 2\,x}$$

The **normal** command acts recursively over functions, sets, and lists.

```
> normal( [ expr, exp(x+1/x) ] );
```

$$[\frac{x^2 - 1}{x\,(x - 2)},\ e^{(\frac{x^2+1}{x})}]$$

```
> big_expr := sin( (x*(x+1)-x)/(x+2) )^2
>             + cos( (x^2)/(-x-2) )^2;
```

$$big\_expr := \sin(\frac{(x + 1)\,x - x}{x + 2})^2 + \cos(\frac{x^2}{-x - 2})^2$$

```
> normal( big_expr );
```

$$\sin(\frac{x^2}{x + 2})^2 + \cos(\frac{x^2}{x + 2})^2$$

Note from the previous example that **normal** does not simplify trigonometric expressions, only rational polynomial functions.

A Special Case Normal may return an expression in expanded form that is not as simple as the factored form.

```
> expr := (x^25-1) / (x-1);
```

$$expr := \frac{x^{25} - 1}{x - 1}$$

```
> normal( expr );
```

$$1 + x^5 + x^4 + x^3 + x^2 + x^{11} + x + x^{16} + x^7 + x^{10} + x^8 + x^6 + x^9$$
$$+ x^{18} + x^{14} + x^{19} + x^{17} + x^{15} + x^{12} + x^{24} + x^{22} + x^{23} + x^{21}$$
$$+ x^{20} + x^{13}$$

To cancel the common $(x - 1)$ term from the numerator and the denominator without expanding the numerator, use **factor**. See this section, page 150.

```
> factor(expr);
```

$$\left(x^4 + x^3 + x^2 + x + 1\right)\left(x^{20} + x^{15} + x^{10} + x^5 + 1\right)$$

Simplifying Expressions

The results of Maple's simplification calculations can be very complicated. The **simplify** command tries to find a simpler expression by applying a list of manipulations.

```
> expr := 4^(1/2) + 3;
```

$$expr := \sqrt{4} + 3$$

```
> simplify( expr );
```

$$5$$

```
> expr := cos(x)^5 + sin(x)^4 + 2*cos(x)^2
>        - 2*sin(x)^2 - cos(2*x);
```

$$expr := \cos(x)^5 + \sin(x)^4 + 2\cos(x)^2 - 2\sin(x)^2 - \cos(2x)$$

```
> simplify( expr );
```

$$\cos(x)^4 \left(\cos(x) + 1 \right)$$

Simplification rules are recognized for trigonometric expressions, logarithmic and exponential expressions, radical expressions, expressions with powers, RootOf expressions, and various special functions.

If you specify a particular simplification rule as an argument to the simplify command, then it uses only that simplification rule (or that class of rules).

```
> expr := ln(3*x) + sin(x)^2 + cos(x)^2;
```

$$expr := \ln(3\,x) + \sin(x)^2 + \cos(x)^2$$

```
> simplify( expr, trig );
```

$$\ln(3\,x) + 1$$

```
> simplify( expr, ln );
```

$$\ln(3) + \ln(x) + \sin(x)^2 + \cos(x)^2$$

```
> simplify( expr );
```

$$\ln(3) + \ln(x) + 1$$

For a list of built-in simplification rules, refer to ?simplify.

Simplification with Assumptions

Maple may not perform a simplification as you would. Although you know that a variable has special properties, Maple treats the variable in a more general way.

```
> expr := sqrt( (x*y)^2 );
```

$$expr := \sqrt{x^2\,y^2}$$

```
> simplify( expr );
```

$$\sqrt{x^2\,y^2}$$

The option `assume=`*property* specifies that `simplify` assume that all the unknowns in the expression have that *property*.

```
> simplify( expr, assume=real );
```

$$|x\,y|$$

```
> simplify( expr, assume=positive );
```

$$x\,y$$

You can also use the general assume facility to place assumptions on individual variables. See section 5.2.

Simplification with Side Relations

Sometimes you can simplify an expression using your own special-purpose transformation rule. The `simplify` command allows you do to this by means of *side relations*.

```
> expr := x*y*z + x*y + x*z + y*z;
```

$$expr := x\,y\,z + x\,y + x\,z + y\,z$$

```
> simplify( expr, { x*z=1 } );
```

$$x\,y + y\,z + y + 1$$

You can give one or more side relations in a set or list. The `simplify` command uses the given equations as additional allowable simplifications.

Specifying the order in which `simplify` performs the simplification provides another level of control.

```
> expr := x^3 + y^3;
```

$$expr := x^3 + y^3$$

```
> siderel := x^2 + y^2 = 1;
```

$$siderel := x^2 + y^2 = 1$$

```
> simplify( expr, {siderel}, [x,y] );
```

$$y^3 - x\,y^2 + x$$

```
> simplify( expr, {siderel}, [y,x] );
```

$$x^3 - y\,x^2 + y$$

In the first case, Maple makes the substitution $x^2 = 1 - y^2$ in the expression, then attempts to make substitutions for y^2 terms. Not finding any, it stops.

In the second case, Maple makes the substitution $y^2 = 1 - x^2$ in the expression, then attempts to make substitutions for x^2 terms. Not finding any, it stops.

Gröbner basis manipulations of polynomials are the basis of how simplify works. For more information, refer to ?simplify,siderels.

Sorting Algebraic Expressions

Maple prints the terms of a polynomial in the order the polynomial was first created. You may want to sort the polynomial by decreasing degree. The sort command makes this possible.

```
> poly := 1 + x^4 - x^2 + x + x^3;
```

$$poly := 1 + x^4 - x^2 + x + x^3$$

```
> sort( poly );
```

$$x^4 + x^3 - x^2 + x + 1$$

Note that sort reorders algebraic expressions in place, replacing the original polynomial with the sorted copy.

```
> poly;
```

$$x^4 + x^3 - x^2 + x + 1$$

You can sort multivariate polynomials in two ways, by total degree or by lexicographic order. The default case is total degree, which sorts terms into descending order of degree. With this sort, if two terms have the same degree, it sorts those terms by lexicographic order (in other words, *a* comes before *b* and so forth).

```
> sort( x+x^3 + w^5 + y^2 + z^4, [w,x,y,z] );
```

$$w^5 + z^4 + x^3 + y^2 + x$$

```
> sort( x^3*y + y^2*x^2, [x,y] );
```

$$x^3 y + x^2 y^2$$

```
> sort( x^3*y + y^2*x^2 + x^4, [x,y] );
```

$$x^4 + x^3 y + x^2 y^2$$

Note that the order of the variables in the list determines the ordering of the expression.

```
> sort( x^3*y + y^2*x^2, [x,y] );
```

$$x^3 y + x^2 y^2$$

```
> sort( x^3*y + y^2*x^2, [y,x] );
```

$$y^2 x^2 + y x^3$$

You can also sort the entire expression by lexicographic ordering, using the **plex** option to the **sort** command.

```
> sort( x + x^3 + w^5 + y^2 + z^4, [w,x,y,z], plex );
```

$$w^5 + x^3 + x + y^2 + z^4$$

Again, the order of the unknowns in the call to **sort** determines the ordering.

```
> sort( x + x^3 + w^5 + y^2 + z^4, [x,y,z,w], plex );
```

$$x^3 + x + y^2 + z^4 + w^5$$

The **sort** command can also sort lists. See section 5.3.

Converting Between Equivalent Forms

You can write many mathematical functions in several equivalent forms. For example, you can express $\sin(x)$ in terms of the exponential function. The `convert` command can perform this and many other types of conversions. For more information, refer to `?convert`.

```
> convert( sin(x), exp );
```

$$\frac{-1}{2} I \left(e^{(x\,I)} - \frac{1}{e^{(x\,I)}} \right)$$

```
> convert( cot(x), sincos );
```

$$\frac{\cos(x)}{\sin(x)}$$

```
> convert( arccos(x), ln );
```

$$-I \ln(x + \sqrt{-x^2 + 1}\, I)$$

```
> convert( binomial(n,k), factorial );
```

$$\frac{n!}{k!\,(n-k)!}$$

The `parfrac` argument indicates partial fractions.

```
> convert( (x^5+1) / (x^4-x^2), parfrac, x );
```

$$x + \frac{1}{x-1} - \frac{1}{x^2}$$

You can also use `convert` to find a fractional *approximation* to a floating-point number.

```
> convert( .3284879342, rational );
```

$$\frac{19615}{59713}$$

Note that conversions are not necessarily mutually inverse.

```
> convert( tan(x), exp );
```

$$\frac{-I\left((e^{(x\,I)})^2 - 1\right)}{(e^{(x\,I)})^2 + 1}$$

```
> convert( %, trig );
```

$$\frac{-I\left((\cos(x) + \sin(x)\,I)^2 - 1\right)}{(\cos(x) + \sin(x)\,I)^2 + 1}$$

The `simplify` command reveals that this expression is $\sin(x)/\cos(x)$, that is, $\tan(x)$.

```
> simplify( % );
```

$$\frac{\sin(x)}{\cos(x)}$$

You can also use the **convert** command to perform structural manipulations on Maple objects. See section 5.3.

5.2   Assumptions

There are two means of imposing assumptions on unknowns. To globally change the properties of unknowns, use the **assume** facility. To perform a single operation under assumptions on unknowns, use the **assuming** command. The **assume** facility and **assuming** command are discussed in the following subsections.

The assume Facility

The *assume facility* is a set of routines for dealing with properties of unknowns. The **assume** command allows improved simplification of symbolic expressions, especially with multiple-valued functions, for example, the square root.

```
> sqrt(a^2);
```

$$\sqrt{a^2}$$

Maple cannot simplify this, as the result is different for positive and negative values of a. Stating an assumption about the value of a allows Maple to simplify the expression.

```
> assume( a>0 );
> sqrt(a^2);
```

$$a^{\sim}$$

The tilde ($^{\sim}$) on a variable indicates that an assumption has been made about it. New assumptions replace old ones.

```
> assume( a<0 );
> sqrt(a^2);
```

$$-a^{\sim}$$

Use the about command to get information about the assumptions on an unknown.

```
> about(a);
```

```
Originally a, renamed a~:
  is assumed to be: RealRange(-infinity,Open(0))
```

Use the additionally command to make additional assumptions about unknowns.

```
> assume(m, nonnegative);
> additionally( m<=0 );
> about(m);
```

```
Originally m, renamed m~:
  is assumed to be: 0
```

Many functions make use of the assumptions on an unknown. The frac command returns the fractional part of a number.

```
> frac(n);
```

$$\mathrm{frac}(n)$$

```
> assume(n, integer);
> frac(n);
```

$$0$$

The following limit depends on b.

```
> limit(b*x, x=infinity);
```

$$\mathrm{signum}(b)\,\infty$$

```
> assume( b>0 );
> limit(b*x, x=infinity);
```

$$\infty$$

You can use `infolevel` to have Maple report the details of command operations.

```
> infolevel[int] := 2;
```

$$infolevel_{int} := 2$$

```
> int( exp(c*x), x=0..infinity );
```

```
int/cook/nogo1:
Given Integral
Int(exp(c*x),x = 0 .. infinity)
Fits into this pattern:
Int(exp(-Ucplex*x^S1-U2*x^S2)*x^N*ln(B*x^DL)^M*cos(C1*x^R)
/((A0+A1*x^D)^P),x = t1 .. t2)
Definite integration: Can't determine if the integral is
convergent.
Need to know the sign of --> -c
Will now try indefinite integration and then take limits.
int/indef1:    first-stage indefinite integration
int/indef2:    second-stage indefinite integration
int/indef2:    applying derivative-divides
int/indef1:    first-stage indefinite integration
```

$$\lim_{x\to\infty}\frac{e^{(cx)}-1}{c}$$

The `int` command must know the sign of `c` (or rather the sign of `-c`).

```
> assume( c>0 );
> int( exp(c*x), x=0..infinity );
```

```
int/cook/nogo1:
Given Integral
Int(exp(x),x = 0 .. infinity)
Fits into this pattern:
Int(exp(-Ucplex*x^S1-U2*x^S2)*x^N*ln(B*x^DL)^M*cos(C1*x^R)
/((A0+A1*x^D)^P),x = t1 .. t2)
int/cook/IIntd1:
--> U must be <= 0 for converging integral
--> will use limit to find if integral is +infinity
--> or - infinity or undefined
```

$$\infty$$

Logarithms are multiple-valued. For general complex values of x, $\ln(e^x)$ is different from x.

```
> ln( exp( 3*Pi*I ) );
```

$$\pi I$$

Therefore, Maple does not simplify the following expression unless it is known to be correct, for example, when x is real.

```
> ln(exp(x));
```

$$\ln(e^x)$$

```
> assume(x, real);
> ln(exp(x));
```

$$x^{\sim}$$

You can use the **is** command to directly test the properties of unknowns.

```
> is( c>0 );
```

$$true$$

```
> is(x, complex);
```

$$true$$

```
> is(x, real);
```

$$true$$

In this next example, Maple still assumes that the variable a is negative.

```
> eq := xi^2 = a;
```

$$eq := \xi^2 = a\tilde{}$$

```
> solve( eq, {xi} );
```

$$\{\xi = \sqrt{-a\tilde{}}\, I\}, \{\xi = -I\,\sqrt{-a\tilde{}}\}$$

To remove assumptions that you make on a name, simply unassign the name. However, the expression eq still refers to a~.

```
> eq;
```

$$\xi^2 = a\tilde{}$$

*You must remove the assumption on **a** inside **eq*** before you remove the assumption on a. First, remove the assumptions on a inside eq.

```
> eq := subs( a='a', eq );
```

$$eq := \xi^2 = a$$

Then, unassign a.

```
> a := 'a';
```

$$a := a$$

For more information on the assume facility, refer to ?assume.

If you require an assumption to hold for only one evaluation, then you can use the assuming command, described in the following subsection. When using the assuming command, you do not need to remove the assumptions on unknowns and equations.

The assuming Command

To perform a single evaluation under assumptions on the name(s) in an expression, use the assuming command. Its use is equivalent to imposing assumptions by using the assume facility, evaluating the expression, then removing the assumptions from the expression and names. This facilitates experimenting with the evaluation of an expression under different assumptions.

```
> about(a);
```

a:
  nothing known about this object

```
> sqrt(a^2) assuming a<0;
```

$$-a$$

```
> about(a);
```

a:
  nothing known about this object

```
> sqrt(a^2) assuming a>0;
```

$$a$$

You can evaluate an expression under an assumption on all names in an expression

```
> sqrt((a*b)^2) assuming positive;
```

$$a\,b^{\sim}$$

or assumption(s) on specific names.

```
> ln(exp(x)) + ln(exp(y)) assuming x::real, y::complex;
```

$$x^{\sim} + \ln(e^y)$$

In this example, the double colon (::) indicates a property assignment. In general, it is used for type checking. For more information, refer to **?type**.

For more information about the **assuming** command, refer to **?assuming**.

5.3   Structural Manipulations

Structural manipulations include selecting and changing parts of an object. They use knowledge of the structure or internal representation of an object rather than working with the expression as a purely mathematical expression. In the special cases of lists and sets, choosing an element is straightforward.

```
> L := { Z, Q, R, C, H, O };
```

$$L := \{O, R, Z, Q, C, H\}$$

```
> L[3];
```

$$Z$$

Selecting elements from lists and sets is easy, which makes manipulating them straightforward. The concept of what constitutes the parts of a general expression is more difficult. However, many of the commands that manipulate lists and sets also apply to general expressions.

Mapping a Function onto a List or Set

You may want to apply a function or command to each of the elements rather than to the object as a whole. The **map** command does this.

```
> f( [a, b, c] );
```

$$f([a, b, c])$$

```
> map( f, [a, b, c] );
```

$$[f(a), f(b), f(c)]$$

```
> map( expand, { (x+1)*(x+2), x*(x+2) } );
```

$$\{x^2 + 2\,x,\ x^2 + 3\,x + 2\}$$

```
> map( x->x^2, [a, b, c] );
```

$$[a^2,\ b^2,\ c^2]$$

If you give `map` more than two arguments, it passes the extra argument(s) to the function.

```
> map( f, [a, b, c], p, q );
```

$$[\mathrm{f}(a,\ p,\ q),\ \mathrm{f}(b,\ p,\ q),\ \mathrm{f}(c,\ p,\ q)]$$

```
> map( diff, [ (x+1)*(x+2), x*(x+2) ], x );
```

$$[2\,x + 3,\ 2\,x + 2]$$

The `map2` command is closely related to `map`. Whereas `map` sequentially replaces the first argument of a function, the `map2` command replaces the second argument to a function.

```
> map2( f, p, [a,b,c], q, r );
```

$$[\mathrm{f}(p,\ a,\ q,\ r),\ \mathrm{f}(p,\ b,\ q,\ r),\ \mathrm{f}(p,\ c,\ q,\ r)]$$

You can use `map2` to list all the partial derivatives of an expression.

```
> map2( diff, x^y/z, [x,y,z] );
```

$$[\frac{x^y\,y}{x\,z},\ \frac{x^y\ln(x)}{z},\ -\frac{x^y}{z^2}]$$

You can use `map2` in conjunction with `map` when applying them to subelements.

```
> map2( map, { [a,b], [c,d], [e,f] }, p, q );
```

$$\{[\mathrm{a}(p,\ q),\ \mathrm{b}(p,\ q)],\ [\mathrm{c}(p,\ q),\ \mathrm{d}(p,\ q)],\ [\mathrm{e}(p,\ q),\ \mathrm{f}(p,\ q)]\}$$

You can also use the **seq** command to generate sequences resembling the output from **map**. In this example, **seq** generates a sequence by applying the function **f** to the elements of a set and a list.

```
> seq( f(i), i={a,b,c} );
```

$$f(a),\ f(b),\ f(c)$$

```
> seq( f(p, i, q, r), i=[a,b,c] );
```

$$f(p,\ a,\ q,\ r),\ f(p,\ b,\ q,\ r),\ f(p,\ c,\ q,\ r)$$

Another example is Pascal's Triangle.

```
> L := [ seq( i, i=0..5 ) ];
```

$$L := [0,\ 1,\ 2,\ 3,\ 4,\ 5]$$

```
> [ seq( [ seq( binomial(n,m), m=L ) ], n=L ) ];
```

$$[[1,\ 0,\ 0,\ 0,\ 0,\ 0],\ [1,\ 1,\ 0,\ 0,\ 0,\ 0],\ [1,\ 2,\ 1,\ 0,\ 0,\ 0],$$
$$[1,\ 3,\ 3,\ 1,\ 0,\ 0],\ [1,\ 4,\ 6,\ 4,\ 1,\ 0],\ [1,\ 5,\ 10,\ 10,\ 5,\ 1]]$$

```
> map( print, % );
```

$$[1,\ 0,\ 0,\ 0,\ 0,\ 0]$$

$$[1,\ 1,\ 0,\ 0,\ 0,\ 0]$$

$$[1,\ 2,\ 1,\ 0,\ 0,\ 0]$$

$$[1,\ 3,\ 3,\ 1,\ 0,\ 0]$$

$$[1,\ 4,\ 6,\ 4,\ 1,\ 0]$$

$$[1,\ 5,\ 10,\ 10,\ 5,\ 1]$$

$$[]$$

The **add** and **mul** commands work like **seq** except that they generate sums and products, respectively, instead of sequences.

```
> add( i^2, i=[5, y, sin(x), -5] );
```

$$50 + y^2 + \sin(x)^2$$

The map, map2, seq, add, and mul commands can also act on general expressions. See this section, pages 169–171.

Choosing Elements from a List or Set

You can select certain elements from a list or a set, if you have a boolean-valued function that determines which elements to select. The following boolean-valued function returns true if its argument is larger than three.

```
> large := x -> is(x > 3);
```

$$large := x \rightarrow \mathrm{is}(3 < x)$$

You can now use the **select** command to choose the elements in a list or set that satisfy large.

```
> L := [ 8, 2.95, Pi, sin(9) ];
```

$$L := [8,\ 2.95,\ \pi,\ \sin(9)]$$

```
> select( large, L );
```

$$[8,\ \pi]$$

Similarly, the **remove** command removes the elements from L that satisfy large and displays as output the remaining elements.

```
> remove( large, L );
```

$$[2.95,\ \sin(9)]$$

To perform both operations simultaneously, use the **selectremove** command.

```
> selectremove( large, L);
```

$$[8,\ \pi],\ [2.95,\ \sin(9)]$$

Use the **type** command to determine the type of an expression.

```
> type( 3, numeric );
```

$$true$$

```
> type( cos(1), numeric );
```

$$false$$

The syntax of **select** here passes the third argument, **numeric**, to the **type** command.

```
> select( type, L, numeric );
```

$$[8, 2.95]$$

See this section, pages 179–185, for more information on types and using **select** and **remove** on a general expression.

Merging Two Lists

Sometimes you need to merge two lists. Here is a list of x-values and a list of y-values.

```
> X := [ seq( ithprime(i), i=1..6 ) ];
```

$$X := [2, 3, 5, 7, 11, 13]$$

```
> Y := [ seq( binomial(6, i), i=1..6 ) ];
```

$$Y := [6, 15, 20, 15, 6, 1]$$

To plot the y-values against the x-values, construct a list of lists: [[x1,y1], [x2,y2], ...]. That is, for each pair of values, construct a two-element list.

```
> pair := (x,y) -> [x, y];
```

$$pair := (x, y) \to [x, y]$$

The **zip** command can merge the lists **X** and **Y** according to the binary function **pair**.

```
> P := zip( pair, X, Y );
```

$$P := [[2, 6], [3, 15], [5, 20], [7, 15], [11, 6], [13, 1]]$$

```
> plot( P );
```

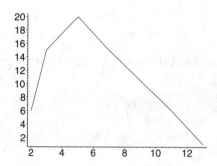

If the two lists have different length, then **zip** returns a list as long as the shorter one.

```
> zip( (x,y) -> x.y, [a,b,c,d,e,f], [1,2,3] );
```

$$[a, 2\,b, 3\,c]$$

You can specify a fourth argument to **zip**. Then **zip** returns a list as long as the longer input list, using the fourth argument for the missing values.

```
> zip( (x,y) -> x.y, [a,b,c,d,e,f], [1,2,3], 99 );
```

$$[a, 2\,b, 3\,c, 99\,d, 99\,e, 99\,f]$$

```
> zip( igcd, [7657,342,876], [34,756,213,346,123], 6! );
```

$$[1, 18, 3, 2, 3]$$

The **zip** command can also merge vectors. For more information, refer to **?zip**.

Sorting Lists

A list is a fundamental order-preserving data structure in Maple. The elements in a list remain in the order used in creating the list. You can create a copy of a list sorted in another order by using the **sort** command.

The **sort** command sorts lists, among other things, in ascending order. It sorts a list of numbers in numerical order.

```
> sort( [1,3,2,4,5,3,6,3,6] );
```

$$[1, 2, 3, 3, 3, 4, 5, 6, 6]$$

The **sort** command also sorts a list of strings in lexicographic order.

```
> sort( ["Mary", "had", "a", "little", "lamb"] );
```

$$[\text{``Mary''}, \text{``a''}, \text{``had''}, \text{``lamb''}, \text{``little''}]$$

If a list contains both numbers and strings, or expressions different from numbers and strings, **sort** uses the machine addresses, which are session dependent.

```
> sort( [x, 1, "apple"] );
```

$$[1, \text{``apple''}, x]$$

```
> sort( [-5, 10, sin(34)] );
```

$$[10, \sin(34), -5]$$

Note that to Maple, π is not numeric.

```
> sort( [4.3, Pi, 2/3] );
```

$$[\pi, 4.3, \frac{2}{3}]$$

You can specify a boolean function to define an ordering for a list. The boolean function must take two arguments and returns **true** if the first argument should precede the second. You can use this to sort a list of numbers in descending order.

```
> sort( [3.12, 1, 1/2], (x,y) -> evalb( x>y ) );
```

$$[3.12, 1, \frac{1}{2}]$$

The `is` command can compare constants like π and $\sin(5)$ with pure numbers.

```
> bf := (x,y) -> is( x < y );
```

$$bf := (x, y) \rightarrow \mathrm{is}(x < y)$$

```
> sort( [4.3, Pi, 2/3, sin(5)], bf );
```

$$[\sin(5), \frac{2}{3}, \pi, 4.3]$$

You can also sort strings by length.

```
> shorter := (x,y) -> evalb( length(x) < length(y) );
```

$$shorter := (x, y) \rightarrow \mathrm{evalb}(\mathrm{length}(x) < \mathrm{length}(y))$$

```
> sort( ["Mary", "has", "a", "little", "lamb"], shorter );
```

$$["a", "has", "lamb", "Mary", "little"]$$

Maple does not have a built-in method for sorting lists of mixed strings and numbers, other than by machine address. To sort a mixed list of strings and numbers, you can do the following.

```
> big_list := [1,"d",3,5,2,"a","c","b",9];
```

$$big\_list := [1, "d", 3, 5, 2, "a", "c", "b", 9]$$

Make two lists from the original, one consisting of numbers and one consisting of strings.

```
> list1 := select( type, big_list, string );
```

$$list1 := ["d", "a", "c", "b"]$$

```
> list2 := select( type, big_list, numeric );
```

$$list2 := [1, 3, 5, 2, 9]$$

Then sort the two lists independently.

```
> list1 := sort(list1);
```

$$list1 := [\text{``a''}, \text{``b''}, \text{``c''}, \text{``d''}]$$

```
> list2 := sort(list2);
```

$$list2 := [1, 2, 3, 5, 9]$$

Finally, stack the two lists together.

```
> sorted_list := [ op(list1), op(list2) ];
```

$$sorted\_list := [\text{``a''}, \text{``b''}, \text{``c''}, \text{``d''}, 1, 2, 3, 5, 9]$$

The **sort** command can also sort algebraic expressions. See section 5.1.

This section, pages 172–173, gives more information about the commands in this example.

The Parts of an Expression

To manipulate the details of an expression, you must select the individual parts. Three easy cases for doing this involve equations, ranges, and fractions. The **lhs** command selects the left-hand side of an equation.

```
> eq := a^2 + b^ 2 = c^2;
```

$$eq := a^2 + b^2 = c^2$$

```
> lhs( eq );
```

$$a^2 + b^2$$

The **rhs** command similarly selects the right-hand side.

```
> rhs( eq );
```

$$c^2$$

The **lhs** and **rhs** commands also work on ranges.

```
> lhs( 2..5 );
```

$$2$$

```
> rhs( 2..5 );
```

$$5$$

```
> eq := x = -2..infinity;
```

$$eq := x = -2..\infty$$

```
> lhs( eq );
```

$$x$$

```
> rhs( eq );
```

$$-2..\infty$$

```
> lhs( rhs(eq) );
```

$$-2$$

```
> rhs( rhs(eq) );
```

$$\infty$$

The **numer** and **denom** commands extract the numerator and denominator, respectively, from a fraction.

```
> numer( 2/3 );
```

$$2$$

```
> denom( 2/3 );
```

$$3$$

```
> fract := ( 1+sin(x)^3-y/x) / ( y^2 - 1 + x );
```

$$fract := \frac{1 + \sin(x)^3 - \dfrac{y}{x}}{y^2 - 1 + x}$$

```
> numer( fract );
```

$$x + \sin(x)^3\, x - y$$

```
> denom( fract );
```

$$x\,(y^2 - 1 + x)$$

Consider the expression

```
> expr := 3 + sin(x) + 2*cos(x)^2*sin(x);
```

$$expr := 3 + \sin(x) + 2\cos(x)^2 \sin(x)$$

The **whattype** command identifies **expr** as a sum.

```
> whattype( expr );
```

$$`+`$$

Use the **op** command to list the terms of a sum or, in general, the operands of an expression.

```
> op( expr );
```

$$3,\ \sin(x),\ 2\cos(x)^2 \sin(x)$$

The expression **expr** consists of three terms. Use the **nops** command to count the number of operands in an expression.

```
> nops( expr );
```

$$3$$

You can select, for example, the third term as follows.

```
> term3 := op(3, expr);
```

$$term3 := 2\cos(x)^2 \sin(x)$$

The expression **term3** is a product of three factors.

```
> whattype( term3 );
```

$$`*`$$

```
> nops( term3 );
```

$$3$$

```
> op( term3 );
```

$$2,\ \cos(x)^2,\ \sin(x)$$

Retrieve the second factor in **term3** in the following manner.

```
> factor2 := op(2, term3);
```

$$factor2 := \cos(x)^2$$

It is an exponentiation.

```
> whattype( factor2 );
```

$$`\wedge`$$

The expression **factor2** has two operands.

```
> op( factor2 );
```

$$\cos(x),\ 2$$

The first operand is a function and has only one operand.

```
> op1 := op(1, factor2);
```

$$op1 := \cos(x)$$

```
> whattype( op1 );
```

function

```
> op( op1 );
```

$$x$$

The name x is a symbol.

```
> whattype( op(op1) );
```

symbol

Since you did not assign a value to x, it has only one operand, namely itself.

```
> nops( x );
```

$$1$$

```
> op( x );
```

$$x$$

You can represent the result of finding the operands of the operands of an expression as a picture called an *expression tree*. The expression tree for **expr** looks like this.

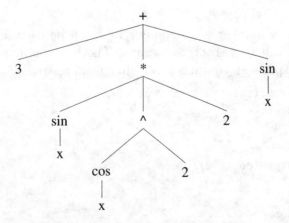

The operands of a list or set are the elements.

```
> op( [a,b,c] );
```

$$a,\, b,\, c$$

```
> op( {d,e,f} );
```

$$e,\, d,\, f$$

This section (page 169) describes how the **map** command applies a function to all the elements of a list or set. The functionality of **map** extends to general expressions.

```
> map( f, x^2 );
```

$$f(x)^{f(2)}$$

The **select** and **remove** commands, described in this section (pages 172–173) also work on general expressions.

```
> large := z -> evalb( is(z>3) = true );
```

$$large := z \rightarrow \mathrm{evalb}(\mathrm{is}(3 < z) = true)$$

```
> remove( large, 5+8*sin(x) - exp(9) );
```

$$8\sin(x) - e^9$$

Maple has a number of commands that can be used as the boolean function in a call to **select** or **remove**. The **has** command determines whether an expression contains a certain subexpression.

```
> has( x*exp(cos(t^2)), t^2 );
```

$$true$$

```
> has( x*exp(cos(t^2)), cos );
```

$$true$$

Some of the solutions to the following set of equations contain **RootOfs**.

```
> sol := { solve( { x^2*y^2 = b*y, x^2-y^2 = a*x },
>                    {x,y} ) };
```

$$sol := \{\{y = 0,\, x = 0\},\, \{y = 0,\, x = a\},\, \{$$
$$y = \frac{b}{\text{RootOf}(\_Z^6 - b^2 - a\_Z^5)^2},$$
$$x = \text{RootOf}(\_Z^6 - b^2 - a\_Z^5)\}\}$$

Use **select** and **has** to choose those solutions.

```
> select( has, sol, RootOf );
```

$$\{\{y = \frac{b}{\text{RootOf}(\_Z^6 - b^2 - a\_Z^5)^2},$$
$$x = \text{RootOf}(\_Z^6 - b^2 - a\_Z^5)\}\}$$

You can also select or remove subexpressions by type. The **type** command determines if an expression is of a certain type.

```
> type( 3+x, '+' );
```

$$true$$

In this example, the **select** command passes its third argument, '+', to **type**.

```
> expr := ( 3+x ) * x^2 * sin( 1+sqrt(Pi) );
```

$$expr := (3 + x)\, x^2 \sin(1 + \sqrt{\pi})$$

```
> select( type, expr, '+' );
```

$$3 + x$$

The **hastype** command determines if an expression contains a subexpression of a certain type.

```
> hastype( sin( 1+sqrt(Pi) ), '+' );
```

$$true$$

Use the combination **select(hastype,...)** to select the operands of an expression that contain a certain type.

```
> select( hastype, expr, '+' );
```

$$(3 + x)\sin(1 + \sqrt{\pi})$$

If you are interested in the subexpressions of a certain type rather than the operands that contain them, use the **indets** command.

```
> indets( expr, '+' );
```

$$\{3 + x,\ 1 + \sqrt{\pi}\}$$

The two **RootOfs** in **sol** above are of type **RootOf**. Since the two **RootOfs** are identical, the set that **indets** returns contains only one element.

```
> indets( sol, RootOf );
```

$$\{\mathrm{RootOf}(\_Z^6 - b^2 - a\,\_Z^5)\}$$

Not all commands are their own type, as is **RootOf**, but you can use the structured type **specfunc(type, name)**. This type matches the function *name* with arguments of type *type*.

```
> type( diff(y(x), x), specfunc(anything, diff) );
```

true

You can use this to find all the derivatives in a large differential equation.

```
> DE := expand( diff( cos(y(t)+t)*sin(t*z(t)), t ) )
>     + diff(x(t), t);
```

$DE := -\sin(t\,z(t))\sin(y(t))\cos(t)\,(\frac{d}{dt}\,y(t))$
$\quad - \sin(t\,z(t))\sin(y(t))\cos(t)$
$\quad - \sin(t\,z(t))\cos(y(t))\sin(t)\,(\frac{d}{dt}\,y(t))$
$\quad - \sin(t\,z(t))\cos(y(t))\sin(t) + \cos(t\,z(t))\cos(y(t))\cos(t)\,z(t)$
$\quad + \cos(t\,z(t))\cos(y(t))\cos(t)\,t\,(\frac{d}{dt}\,z(t))$
$\quad - \cos(t\,z(t))\sin(y(t))\sin(t)\,z(t)$
$\quad - \cos(t\,z(t))\sin(y(t))\sin(t)\,t\,(\frac{d}{dt}\,z(t)) + (\frac{d}{dt}\,x(t))$

```
> indets( DE, specfunc(anything, diff) );
```

$$\{\frac{d}{dt}\,y(t),\ \frac{d}{dt}\,x(t),\ \frac{d}{dt}\,z(t)\}$$

The following operands of DE contain the derivatives.

```
> select( hastype, DE, specfunc(anything, diff) );
```

$$-\sin(t\,z(t))\sin(y(t))\cos(t)\,(\tfrac{d}{dt}\,y(t))$$
$$- \sin(t\,z(t))\cos(y(t))\sin(t)\,(\tfrac{d}{dt}\,y(t))$$
$$+ \cos(t\,z(t))\cos(y(t))\cos(t)\,t\,(\tfrac{d}{dt}\,z(t))$$
$$- \cos(t\,z(t))\sin(y(t))\sin(t)\,t\,(\tfrac{d}{dt}\,z(t)) + (\tfrac{d}{dt}\,x(t))$$

DE has only one operand that is itself a derivative.

```
> select( type, DE, specfunc(anything, diff) );
```

$$\frac{d}{dt}\,x(t)$$

Maple recognizes many types. For a partial list, refer to **?type** and for more information on structured types, such as **specfunc**, refer to **?type,structured**.

Substitution

Often you want to substitute a value for a variable (that is, evaluate an expression at a point). For example, if you need to solve the problem, "If $f(x) = \ln(\sin(xe^{\cos(x)}))$, find $f'(2)$," then you must substitute the value 2 for x in the derivative. The command finds the derivative.

```
> y := ln( sin( x * exp(cos(x)) ) );
```

$$y := \ln(\sin(x\,e^{\cos(x)}))$$

```
> yprime := diff( y, x );
```

$$yprime := \frac{\cos(x\,e^{\cos(x)})\,(e^{\cos(x)} - x\sin(x)\,e^{\cos(x)})}{\sin(x\,e^{\cos(x)})}$$

Now use the **eval** command to substitute a value for **x** in **yprime**.

```
> eval( yprime, x=2 );
```

$$\frac{\cos(2\,e^{\cos(2)})\,(e^{\cos(2)} - 2\sin(2)\,e^{\cos(2)})}{\sin(2\,e^{\cos(2)})}$$

The **evalf** command returns a floating-point approximation of the result.

```
> evalf( % );
```

$$-0.1388047428$$

The command makes syntactical substitutions, not mathematical substitutions. This means that you can make substitutions for any subexpression.

```
> subs( cos(x)=3, yprime );
```

$$\frac{\cos(x\,e^{3})\,(e^{3} - x\sin(x)\,e^{3})}{\sin(x\,e^{3})}$$

But you are limited to subexpressions as Maple identifies them.

```
> expr := a * b * c * a^b;
```

$$expr := a\,b\,c\,a^{b}$$

```
> subs( a*b=3, expr );
```

$$a\,b\,c\,a^{b}$$

expr is a product of four factors.

```
> op( expr );
```

$$a, \, b, \, c, \, a^b$$

The product **a*b** is not a factor in **expr**. You can make the substitution **a*b=3** in three ways: solve the subexpression for one of the variables,

```
> subs( a=3/b, expr );
```

$$3 \, c \left(\frac{3}{b}\right)^b$$

use a side relation to **simplify**,

```
> simplify( expr, { a*b=3 } );
```

$$3 \, c \, a^b$$

or use the **algsubs** command, which performs algebraic substitutions.

```
> algsubs( a*b=3, expr);
```

$$3 \, c \, a^b$$

Note that in the first case all occurrences of **a** have been replaced by **3/b**. Whereas, in the second and third cases both variables **a** and **b** remain in the result.

You can make several substitutions with one call to **subs**.

```
> expr := z * sin( x^2 ) + w;
```

$$expr := z \sin(x^2) + w$$

```
> subs( x=sqrt(z), w=Pi, expr );
```

$$z \sin(z) + \pi$$

The **subs** command makes the substitutions from left to right.

```
> subs( z=x, x=sqrt(z), expr );
```

$$\sqrt{z}\sin(z) + w$$

If you give a set or list of substitutions, **subs** makes those substitutions simultaneously.

```
> subs( { x=sqrt(Pi), z=3 }, expr );
```

$$3\sin(\pi) + w$$

Note that in general you must explicitly evaluate the result of a call to **subs**.

```
> eval( % );
```

$$w$$

Use the **subsop** command to substitute for a specific operand of an expression.

```
> expr := 5^x;
```

$$expr := 5^x$$

```
> op( expr );
```

$$5,\, x$$

```
> subsop( 1=t, expr );
```

$$t^x$$

The zeroth operand of a function is typically the name of the function.

```
> expr := cos(x);
```

$$expr := \cos(x)$$

```
> subsop( 0=sin, expr );
```

$$\sin(x)$$

This section, pages 177–182, explains the operands of an expression.

Changing the Type of an Expression

You may find it necessary to convert an expression to another type. Consider the Taylor series for $\sin(x)$.

```
> f := sin(x);
```

$$f := \sin(x)$$

```
> t := taylor( f, x=0 );
```

$$t := x - \frac{1}{6}x^3 + \frac{1}{120}x^5 + \mathrm{O}(x^6)$$

For example, you cannot plot a series, you must use `convert(...,` `polynom)` to convert it into a polynomial approximation first.

```
> p := convert( t, polynom );
```

$$p := x - \frac{1}{6}x^3 + \frac{1}{120}x^5$$

Similarly, the title of a plot must be a string, not a general expression. You can use `convert(..., string)` to convert an expression to a string.

```
> p_txt := convert( p, string );
```

$$p\_txt := \text{``x-1/6*x^3+1/120*x^ 5''}$$

```
> plot( p, x=-4..4, title=p_txt );
```

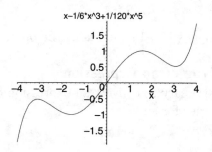

The **cat** command concatenates all its arguments to create a new string.

```
> ttl := cat( convert( f, string ),
>              " and its Taylor approximation ",
>              p_txt );
```

$ttl :=$ "sin(x) and its Taylor approximation x-1/6*x^\
3+1/120*x^5"

```
> plot( [f, p], x=-4..4, title=ttl );
```

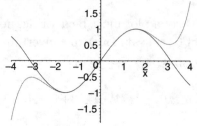

You can also convert a list to a set or a set to a list.

```
> L := [1,2,5,2,1];
```

$$L := [1, 2, 5, 2, 1]$$

```
> S := convert( L, set );
```

$$S := \{1, 2, 5\}$$

```
> convert( S, list );
```

$$[1, 2, 5]$$

The `convert` command can perform many other structural and mathematical conversions. For more information, refer to `?convert`.

5.4 Evaluation Rules

In a symbolic mathematics program such as Maple you encounter the issue of *evaluation*. If you assign the value y to x, the value z to y, and the value 5 to z, then to what should x evaluate?

Levels of Evaluation

Maple, in most cases, does full evaluation of names. That is, when you use a name or symbol, Maple checks if the name or symbol has an assigned value. If it has a value, Maple substitutes the value for the name. If this value itself has an assigned value, Maple performs a substitution again, and so on, recursively, until no more substitutions are possible.

```
> x := y;
```

$$x := y$$

```
> y := z;
```

$$y := z$$

```
> z := 5;
```

$$z := 5$$

Now Maple evaluates x fully. That is, Maple substitutes y for x, z for y, and finally, 5 for z.

```
> x;
```

$$5$$

You can use the `eval` command to control the level of evaluation of an expression. If you call `eval` with just one argument, then `eval` evaluates that argument fully.

```
> eval(x);
```

$$5$$

A second argument to `eval` specifies how far you want to evaluate the first argument.

```
> eval(x, 1);
```

$$y$$

```
> eval(x, 2);
```

$$z$$

```
> eval(x, 3);
```

$$5$$

The main exceptions to the rule of full evaluation are special data structures like tables, matrices, and procedures, and the behavior of local variables inside a procedure.

Last-Name Evaluation

The data structures `array`, `table`, `matrix`, and `proc` have a special evaluation behavior called *last-name evaluation*.

```
> x := y;
```

$$x := y$$

```
> y := z;
```

$$y := z$$

```
> z := array( [ [1,2], [3,4] ] );
```

$$z := \begin{bmatrix} 1 & 2 \\ 3 & 4 \end{bmatrix}$$

Maple substitutes y for x and z for y. Because evaluation of the last name, z, would produce an array, one of the four special structures, z is unevaluated.

```
> x;
```

$$z$$

Maple uses last-name evaluation for arrays, tables, matrices, and procedures to retain compact representations of unassigned table entries (for example, T[3]) and unevaluated commands (for example, sin(x)). For more information on last-name evaluation, refer to ?last_name_eval. You can force full evaluation by calling eval explicitly.

```
> eval(x);
```

$$\begin{bmatrix} 1 & 2 \\ 3 & 4 \end{bmatrix}$$

```
> add2 := proc(x,y) x+y; end proc;
```

$$add2 := \mathbf{proc}(x, y)\, x + y\, \mathbf{end\ proc}$$

```
> add2;
```

$$add2$$

You can easily force full evaluation, using eval or print.

```
> eval(add2);
```

$$\mathbf{proc}(x, y)\, x + y\, \mathbf{end\ proc}$$

Note that full evaluation of Maple library procedures, by default, suppresses the code in the procedure. To illustrate this, examine the **erfi** command

```
> erfi;
```

$$erfi$$

```
> eval(erfi);
```

$$\mathbf{proc}(x\text{::}algebraic) \ldots \mathbf{end\ proc}$$

Set the `interface` variable **verboseproc** to 2, and then try again.

```
> interface( verboseproc=2 );
> eval(erfi);
```

proc(x::*algebraic*)
option'*Copyright (c) 1996 Waterloo Maple Inc. Al*
l rights reserved.';
  if nargs $\neq 1$ **then**
    error "expecting 1 argument, got %1", nargs
  elif type(x, 'complex(*float*)') **then** evalf('*erfi*'(x))
  elif $x = 0$ **then** 0
  elif type(x, '∞') **then**
    if type(x, '*cx_infinity*') **then** *undefined* + *undefined* $* I$
    elif type(x, '*undefined*') **then**
      NumericTools : $- ThrowUndefined$(x)
    elif type(x, '*extended_numeric*') **then** x
    elif type($\Re(x)$, '∞') **then** $\infty + \infty * I$
    else CopySign(I, $\Im(x)$)
    end if
  elif type(x, '*undefined*') **then**
    NumericTools : $- ThrowUndefined$(x, '*preserve*' = '*axes*')
  elif type(x, '$*$') **and** member(I, {op(x)}) **then** erf($-I * x$) $* I$
  elif type(x, 'complex(*numeric*)') **and** csgn(x) < 0 **then**
    $-$ erfi($-x$)
  elif type(x, '$*$') **and** type(op(1, x), 'complex(*numeric*)')
    and csgn(op(1, x)) < 0**then** $-$ erfi($-x$)
  elif type(x, '$+$') **and** traperror(sign(x)) $= -1$ **then** $-$ erfi($-x$)
  else '*erfi*'(x)
  end if
end proc

The default value of `verboseproc` is 1.

```
> interface( verboseproc=1 );
```
The help page `?interface` explains the possible settings of `verboseproc` and the other `interface` variables.

One-Level Evaluation

Local variables of a procedure use one-level evaluation. That is, if you assign a local variable, then the result of evaluation is the value most recently assigned directly to that variable.

```
> test:=proc()
>    local x, y, z;
```

```
>    x := y;
>    y := z;
>    z := 5;
>    x;
> end proc:
> test();
```

$$y$$

Compare this evaluation with the similar interactive example in this section on page 191. Full evaluation within a procedure is rarely necessary and can lead to inefficiency. If you require full evaluation within a procedure, use eval.

Commands with Special Evaluation Rules

The assigned **and** evaln **Commands**   The functions assigned and evaln evaluate their arguments only to the level at which they become names.

```
> x := y;
```

$$x := y$$

```
> y := z;
```

$$y := z$$

```
> evaln(x);
```

$$x$$

The assigned command checks if a name has a value assigned to it.

```
> assigned( x );
```

true

The seq **Command**   The seq command for creating expression sequences does not evaluate its arguments, so that even if a variable has an assigned value, seq can use it as a counting variable.

```
> i := 2;
```

$$i := 2$$

```
> seq( i^2, i=1..5 );
```

$$1, 4, 9, 16, 25$$

```
> i;
```

$$2$$

Contrast this with the behavior of **sum**.

```
> sum( i^2, i=1..5 );
```

```
Error, (in sum) summation variable previously assigned,
second argument evaluates to 2 = 1 .. 5
```

You can easily solve this problem using right single quotes, as shown in the next section.

Quotation and Unevaluation

The Maple language supports the use of quotes to delay evaluation one level. Surrounding a name in right single quotes (') prevents Maple from evaluating the name. Hence, right single quotes are referred to as *unevaluation quotes*.

```
> i := 4;
```

$$i := 4$$

```
> i;
```

$$4$$

```
> 'i';
```

$$i$$

Use this method to avoid the following problem.

```
> i;
```

$$4$$

```
> sum( i^2, i=1..5 );
```

Error, (in sum) summation variable previously assigned,
second argument evaluates to 4 = 1 .. 5

```
> sum( 'i^2', 'i'=1..5 );
```

$$55$$

```
> i;
```

$$4$$

Full evaluation of a quoted expression removes one level of quotes.

```
> x := 0;
```

$$x := 0$$

```
> '''x'+1'';
```

$$"x' + 1'$$

```
> %;
```

$$'x' + 1$$

```
> %;
```

$$x + 1$$

```
> %;
```

$$1$$

Quoting an expression delays evaluation, but does not prevent automatic simplifications and arithmetic.

```
> '1-1';
```

$$0$$

```
> 'p+q-i-p+3*q';
```

$$4\,q - i$$

If you enclose a simple variable in right single quotes, the result is the name of the variable. You can use this method to unassign a variable.

```
> x := 1;
```

$$x := 1$$

```
> x;
```

$$1$$

```
> x := 'x';
```

$$x := x$$

```
> x;
```

$$x$$

However, in general, you must use **evaln**.

```
> i := 4;
```

$$i := 4$$

```
> a[i] := 9;
```

$$a_4 := 9$$

Note that `'a[i]'` is `a[i]` not `a[4]`.

```
> 'a[i]';
```

$$a_i$$

You must use `evaln` to unassign `a[i]`.

```
> evaln( a[i] );
```

$$a_4$$

```
> a[i] := evaln( a[i] );
```

$$a_4 := a_4$$

Using Quoted Variables as Function Arguments

Some Maple commands use names as a way to return information in addition to the standard return value. The `divide` command assigns the quotient to the global name, q.

```
> divide( x^2-1, x-1, 'q' );
```

$$true$$

```
> q;
```

$$x + 1$$

Remember to use a quoted name to ensure that you are not passing a variable with an assigned value into the procedure. You can avoid the need for quotes if you ensure that the name you use has no previously assigned value.

```
> q := 2;
```

$$q := 2$$

```
> divide( x^2-y^2, x-y, q );
```

```
Error, wrong number (or type) of parameters in function
divide
```

```
> q := evaln(q);
```

$$q := q$$

```
> divide( x^2-y^2, x-y, q );
```

$$true$$

```
> q;
```

$$x + y$$

The `rem`, `quo`, `irem`, and `iquo` commands behave in a similar manner.

Concatenation of Names

Concatenation is a way to form new variable names based on others.

```
> a||b;
```

$$ab$$

The concatenation operator, "||", in a name causes evaluation of the right-hand side of the operator, but not the left.

```
> a := x;
```

$$a := x$$

```
> b := 2;
```

$$b := 2$$

```
> a||b;
```

$$a2$$

```
> c := 3;
```

$$c := 3$$

```
> a||b||c;
```

$$a23$$

If a name does not evaluate to a single symbol, Maple does not evaluate a concatenation.

```
> a := x;
```

$$a := x$$

```
> b := y+1;
```

$$b := y + 1$$

```
> new_name := a||b;
```

$$new\_name := a||(y+1)$$

```
> y := 3;
```

$$y := 3$$

```
> new_name;
```

$$a4$$

You can use concatenated names to assign and create expressions.

```
> i := 1;
```

$$i := 1$$

```
> b||i := 0;
```

$$b1 := 0$$

You need to use right single quotes.

```
> sum( 'a||k' * x^k, k=0..8 );
```

$$a0 + a1\,x + a2\,x^2 + a3\,x^3 + a4\,x^4 + a5\,x^5 + a6\,x^6 + a7\,x^7$$
$$+\, a8\,x^8$$

If you do not use right single quotes, Maple evaluates `a||k` to `ak`.

```
> sum( a||k * x^k, k=0..8 );
```

$$ak + ak\,x + ak\,x^2 + ak\,x^3 + ak\,x^4 + ak\,x^5 + ak\,x^6 + ak\,x^7$$
$$+\, ak\,x^8$$

You can also use concatenation to form title strings for plots.

5.5   Conclusion

In this chapter, you have seen how to perform many kinds of expression manipulations, from adding two equations to selecting individual parts of a general expression. In general, no rule specifies which form of an expression is the simplest. But, the commands you have seen in this chapter allow you to convert an expression to many forms, often the ones *you* would consider simplest. If not, you can use side relations to specify your own simplification rules, or assumptions to specify properties of unknowns.

You have also seen that Maple, in most cases, uses full evaluation of variables. Some exceptions exist, which include last-name evaluation for certain data structures, one-level evaluation for local variables in a procedure, and delayed evaluation for names in right single quotes.

6   Examples from Calculus

This chapter provides examples of how Maple can help you present and solve problems from calculus. The first section describes elementary concepts such as the derivative and the integral, the second section discusses ordinary differential equations in some depth, and the third section concerns partial differential equations.

6.1   Introductory Calculus

This section contains a number of examples of how to illustrate ideas and solve problems from calculus. The Student[Calculus1] package contains many commands that are especially useful in this area.

The Derivative

This section illustrates the graphical meaning of the derivative: the slope of the tangent line. Then it shows you how to find the set of inflection points for a function.

Define the function $f: x \mapsto \exp(\sin(x))$ in the following manner.

```
> f := x -> exp( sin(x) );
```

$$f := x \to e^{\sin(x)}$$

Find the derivative of f evaluated at $x_0 = 1$.

```
> x0 := 1;
```

$$x0 := 1$$

p_0 and p_1 are two points on the graph of f.

```
> p0 := [ x0, f(x0) ];
```

$$p0 := [1,\, e^{\sin(1)}]$$

```
> p1 := [ x0+h, f(x0+h) ];
```

$$p1 := [1 + h,\, e^{\sin(1+h)}]$$

The NewtonQuotient command from the Student package finds the slope of the secant line through p_0 and p_1.

```
> with(Student[Calculus1]):
```
Use NewtonQuotient command to find the expression for the slope.

```
> m := NewtonQuotient(f(x), x=x0, h=h);
```

$$m := \frac{e^{\sin(1+h)} - e^{\sin(1)}}{h}$$

If $h = 1$, the slope is

```
> eval(%, h=1);
```

$$e^{\sin(2)} - e^{\sin(1)}$$

The evalf command gives a floating-point approximation.

```
> evalf( % );
```

$$0.162800903$$

As h tends to zero, the secant slope values seem to converge.

```
> h_values := seq( NewtonQuotient( f(x), x=1.0, h=1.0/i^2 ),
>                  i=1..20);
```

$h\_values := 0.1628009030,\ 1.053234748,\ 1.174305789,$
$1.210917616,\ 1.226806975,\ 1.235154852,\ 1.240091510,$
$1.243256512,\ 1.245408615,\ 1.246939100,\ 1.248066842,$
$1.248921648,\ 1.249585493,\ 1.250111128,\ 1.250534250,$
$1.250880512,\ 1.251167122,\ 1.251406908,\ 1.251609743,$
1.251782800

The following is the equation of the secant line.

```
> y - p0[2] = m * ( x - p0[1] );
```

$$y - e^{\sin(1)} = \frac{\left(e^{\sin(1+h)} - e^{\sin(1)}\right)(x-1)}{h}$$

The `isolate` command converts the equation to slope–intercept form.

```
> isolate( %, y );
```

$$y = \frac{\left(e^{\sin(1+h)} - e^{\sin(1)}\right)(x-1)}{h} + e^{\sin(1)}$$

You must convert the equation to a function.

```
> secant := unapply( rhs(%), x );
```

$$secant := x \rightarrow \frac{\left(e^{\sin(1+h)} - e^{\sin(1)}\right)(x-1)}{h} + e^{\sin(1)}$$

You can now plot the secant and the function for different values of h. First, make a sequence of plots.

```
> S := seq( plot( [f(x), secant(x)], x=0..4,
>                 view=[0..4, 0..4] ),
>           h=h_values ):
```

The `display` command from the `plots` package can display the plots in sequence, that is, as an animation.

```
> with(plots):
```

```
Warning, the name changecoords has been redefined
```

```
> display( S, insequence=true, view=[0..4, 0..4] );
```

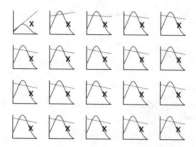

In the limit as h tends to zero, the slope is

> Limit(m, h=0);

$$\lim_{h \to 0} \frac{e^{\sin(1+h)} - e^{\sin(1)}}{h}$$

The value of this limit is

> value(%);

$$e^{\sin(1)} \cos(1)$$

This answer is, of course, the value of $f'(x0)$. To see this, first define the function $f1$ to be the first derivative of f. Since f is a function, use **D**. The **D** operator computes derivatives of functions, while **diff** computes derivatives of expressions. For more information, refer to **?operators,D**.

> f1 := D(f);

$$f1 := x \to \cos(x)\, e^{\sin(x)}$$

Now you can see that $f1(x0)$ equals the limit above.

> f1(x0);

$$e^{\sin(1)} \cos(1)$$

In this case, the second derivative exists.

> diff(f(x), x, x);

$$-\sin(x)\, e^{\sin(x)} + \cos(x)^2\, e^{\sin(x)}$$

Define the function $f2$ to be the second derivative of f.

```
> f2 := unapply( %, x );
```

$$f2 := x \rightarrow -\sin(x)\, e^{\sin(x)} + \cos(x)^2\, e^{\sin(x)}$$

When you plot f and its first and second derivatives, you can see that f is increasing whenever $f1$ is positive, and that f is concave down whenever $f2$ is negative.

```
> plot( [f(x), f1(x), f2(x)], x=0..10 );
```

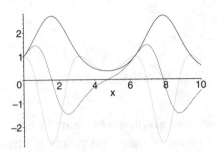

The graph of f has an inflection point where the second derivative changes sign, and the second derivative can change sign at the values of x where $f2(x)$ is zero.

```
> sol := { solve( f2(x)=0, x ) };
```

$$sol := \left\{ \arctan\left(2\,\frac{\frac{1}{2}\sqrt{5} - \frac{1}{2}}{\sqrt{-2 + 2\sqrt{5}}} \right),\ -\arctan\left(2\,\frac{\frac{1}{2}\sqrt{5} - \frac{1}{2}}{\sqrt{-2 + 2\sqrt{5}}} \right) + \pi, \right.$$

$$\arctan(-\frac{1}{2} - \frac{1}{2}\sqrt{5},\ -\frac{1}{2}\sqrt{-2 - 2\sqrt{5}}),$$

$$\left. \arctan(-\frac{1}{2} - \frac{1}{2}\sqrt{5},\ \frac{1}{2}\sqrt{-2 - 2\sqrt{5}}) \right\}$$

Two of these solutions are complex.

```
> evalf( sol );
```

$$\{-1.570796327 + 1.061275064\,I,$$
$$-1.570796327 - 1.061275064\,I, \ 0.6662394321,$$
$$2.475353222\}$$

In this example, only the real solutions are of interest. You can use the **select** command to select the real constants from the solution set.

```
> infl := select( type, sol, realcons );
```

$$infl := \left\{ \arctan\left(2\,\frac{\frac{1}{2}\sqrt{5} - \frac{1}{2}}{\sqrt{-2 + 2\sqrt{5}}}\right), \ -\arctan\left(2\,\frac{\frac{1}{2}\sqrt{5} - \frac{1}{2}}{\sqrt{-2 + 2\sqrt{5}}}\right) + \pi \right\}$$

```
> evalf( infl );
```

$$\{0.6662394321, \ 2.475353222\}$$

You can see from the graph above that $f2$ actually does change sign at these x-values. The set of inflection points is given by the following.

```
> { seq( [x, f(x)], x=infl ) };
```

$$\left\{ \left[\arctan\left(2\,\frac{\frac{1}{2}\sqrt{5} - \frac{1}{2}}{\sqrt{-2 + 2\sqrt{5}}}\right), \ e^{\left(2\,\frac{1/2\sqrt{5}-1/2}{\sqrt{-2+2\sqrt{5}}\sqrt{1+4\frac{(1/2\sqrt{5}-1/2)^2}{-2+2\sqrt{5}}}}\right)}\right], \right.$$

$$\left. \left[-\arctan\left(2\,\frac{\frac{1}{2}\sqrt{5} - \frac{1}{2}}{\sqrt{-2 + 2\sqrt{5}}}\right) + \pi, \ e^{\left(2\,\frac{1/2\sqrt{5}-1/2}{\sqrt{-2+2\sqrt{5}}\sqrt{1+4\frac{(1/2\sqrt{5}-1/2)^2}{-2+2\sqrt{5}}}}\right)}\right] \right\}$$

```
> evalf( % );
```

$$\{[0.6662394321, \ 1.855276958],$$
$$[2.475353222, \ 1.855276958]\}$$

Since f is periodic, it has, of course, infinitely many inflection points. You can obtain these by shifting the two inflection points above horizontally by integer multiples of 2π.

A Taylor Approximation

This section illustrates how you can use Maple to analyze the error term in a Taylor approximation. The following is Taylor's formula.

```
> taylor( f(x), x=a );
```

$$f(a) + D(f)(a)(x-a) + \frac{1}{2}(D^{(2)})(f)(a)(x-a)^2 + \frac{1}{6}(D^{(3)})(f)(a)$$
$$(x-a)^3 + \frac{1}{24}(D^{(4)})(f)(a)(x-a)^4 + \frac{1}{120}(D^{(5)})(f)(a)(x-a)^5 +$$
$$O((x-a)^6)$$

You can use it to find a polynomial approximation of a function f near $x = a$.

```
> f := x -> exp( sin(x) );
```

$$f := x \to e^{\sin(x)}$$

```
> a := Pi;
```

$$a := \pi$$

```
> taylor( f(x), x=a );
```

$$1 - (x-\pi) + \frac{1}{2}(x-\pi)^2 - \frac{1}{8}(x-\pi)^4 + \frac{1}{15}(x-\pi)^5 + O((x-\pi)^6)$$

Before you can plot the Taylor approximation, you must convert it from a series to a polynomial.

```
> poly := convert( %, polynom );
```

$$poly := 1 - x + \pi + \frac{1}{2}(x-\pi)^2 - \frac{1}{8}(x-\pi)^4 + \frac{1}{15}(x-\pi)^5$$

Now plot the function f along with `poly`.

```
> plot( [f(x), poly], x=0..10, view=[0..10, 0..3] );
```

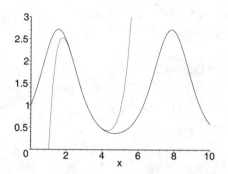

The expression $(1/6!)f^{(6)}(\xi)(x-a)^6$ gives the error of the approximation, where ξ is some number between x and a. The sixth derivative of f is

```
> diff( f(x), x$6 );
```

$$-\sin(x)\,e^{\sin(x)} + 16\cos(x)^2\,e^{\sin(x)} - 15\sin(x)^2\,e^{\sin(x)}$$
$$+ 75\sin(x)\cos(x)^2\,e^{\sin(x)} - 20\cos(x)^4\,e^{\sin(x)} - 15\sin(x)^3\,e^{\sin(x)}$$
$$+ 45\sin(x)^2\cos(x)^2\,e^{\sin(x)} - 15\sin(x)\cos(x)^4\,e^{\sin(x)}$$
$$+ \cos(x)^6\,e^{\sin(x)}$$

The use of the sequence operator $ in the previous command allows you to abbreviate the calling sequence. Otherwise, you are required to enter , x six times to calculate the sixth derivative. Define the function $f6$ to be that derivative.

```
> f6 := unapply( %, x );
```

$$f6 := x \rightarrow -\sin(x)\,e^{\sin(x)} + 16\cos(x)^2\,e^{\sin(x)} - 15\sin(x)^2\,e^{\sin(x)}$$
$$+ 75\sin(x)\cos(x)^2\,e^{\sin(x)} - 20\cos(x)^4\,e^{\sin(x)} - 15\sin(x)^3\,e^{\sin(x)}$$
$$+ 45\sin(x)^2\cos(x)^2\,e^{\sin(x)} - 15\sin(x)\cos(x)^4\,e^{\sin(x)}$$
$$+ \cos(x)^6\,e^{\sin(x)}$$

The following is the error in the approximation.

```
> err := 1/6! * f6(xi) * (x - a)^6;
```

$$err := \frac{1}{720}(-\sin(\xi)\,e^{\sin(\xi)} + 16\cos(\xi)^2\,e^{\sin(\xi)} - 15\sin(\xi)^2\,e^{\sin(\xi)}$$
$$+ 75\sin(\xi)\cos(\xi)^2\,e^{\sin(\xi)} - 20\cos(\xi)^4\,e^{\sin(\xi)} - 15\sin(\xi)^3\,e^{\sin(\xi)}$$
$$+ 45\sin(\xi)^2\cos(\xi)^2\,e^{\sin(\xi)} - 15\sin(\xi)\cos(\xi)^4\,e^{\sin(\xi)}$$
$$+ \cos(\xi)^6\,e^{\sin(\xi)})(x - \pi)^6$$

The previous plot indicates that the error is small (in absolute value) for x between 2 and 4.

```
> plot3d( abs( err ), x=2..4, xi=2..4,
>     style=patch, axes=boxed );
```

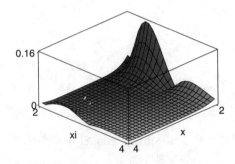

To find the size of the error, you need a full analysis of the expression **err** for x between 2 and 4 and ξ between a and x, that is, on the two closed regions bounded by $x = 2$, $x = 4$, $\xi = a$, and $\xi = x$. The **curve** command from the **plottools** package can illustrate these two regions.

```
> with(plots): with(plottools):

Warning, the name changecoords has been redefined
Warning, the name arrow has been redefined


> display( curve( [ [2,2], [2,a], [4,a], [4,4], [2,2] ] ),
>           labels=[x, xi] );
```

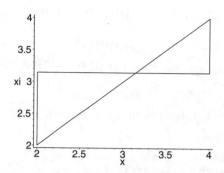

The partial derivatives of **err** help you find extrema of **err** inside the two regions. Then you need to check the four boundaries. The two partial derivatives of **err** are

```
> err_x := diff(err, x);
```

$$err\_x := \frac{1}{120}(-\sin(\xi)\,e^{\sin(\xi)} + 16\cos(\xi)^2\,e^{\sin(\xi)}$$
$$- 15\sin(\xi)^2\,e^{\sin(\xi)} + 75\sin(\xi)\cos(\xi)^2\,e^{\sin(\xi)} - 20\cos(\xi)^4\,e^{\sin(\xi)}$$
$$- 15\sin(\xi)^3\,e^{\sin(\xi)} + 45\sin(\xi)^2\cos(\xi)^2\,e^{\sin(\xi)}$$
$$- 15\sin(\xi)\cos(\xi)^4\,e^{\sin(\xi)} + \cos(\xi)^6\,e^{\sin(\xi)})(x - \pi)^5$$

```
> err_xi := diff(err, xi);
```

$$err\_xi := \frac{1}{720}(-\cos(\xi)\,e^{\sin(\xi)} - 63\sin(\xi)\cos(\xi)\,e^{\sin(\xi)}$$
$$+ 91\cos(\xi)^3\,e^{\sin(\xi)} - 210\sin(\xi)^2\cos(\xi)\,e^{\sin(\xi)}$$
$$+ 245\sin(\xi)\cos(\xi)^3\,e^{\sin(\xi)} - 35\cos(\xi)^5\,e^{\sin(\xi)}$$
$$- 105\sin(\xi)^3\cos(\xi)\,e^{\sin(\xi)} + 105\sin(\xi)^2\cos(\xi)^3\,e^{\sin(\xi)}$$
$$- 21\sin(\xi)\cos(\xi)^5\,e^{\sin(\xi)} + \cos(\xi)^7\,e^{\sin(\xi)})(x - \pi)^6$$

The two partial derivatives are zero at a critical point.

```
> sol := solve( {err_x=0, err_xi=0}, {x, xi} );
```

$$sol := \{x = \pi, \xi = \xi\}$$

The error is zero at this critical point.

```
> eval( err, sol );
```

$$0$$

You need to collect a set of critical values. The largest critical value then bounds the maximal error.

```
> critical := { % };
```

$$critical := \{0\}$$

The partial derivative err_xi is zero at a critical point on either of the two boundaries at $x = 2$ and $x = 4$.

```
> sol := { solve( err_xi=0, xi ) };
```

$$sol := \{\frac{1}{2}\pi, \arctan(\text{RootOf}(\%1, index = 4),$$
$$\text{RootOf}(\_Z^2 + \text{RootOf}(\%1, index = 4)^2 - 1)), \arctan($$
$$\text{RootOf}(\%1, index = 1),$$
$$\text{RootOf}(\_Z^2 + \text{RootOf}(\%1, index = 1)^2 - 1)), \arctan($$
$$\text{RootOf}(\%1, index = 5),$$
$$\text{RootOf}(\_Z^2 + \text{RootOf}(\%1, index = 5)^2 - 1)), \arctan($$
$$\text{RootOf}(\%1, index = 2),$$
$$\text{RootOf}(\_Z^2 + \text{RootOf}(\%1, index = 2)^2 - 1)), \arctan($$
$$\text{RootOf}(\%1, index = 6),$$
$$\text{RootOf}(\_Z^2 + \text{RootOf}(\%1, index = 6)^2 - 1)), \arctan($$
$$\text{RootOf}(\%1, index = 3),$$
$$\text{RootOf}(\_Z^2 + \text{RootOf}(\%1, index = 3)^2 - 1))\}$$
$$\%1 := -56 - 161\_Z + 129\_Z^2 + 308\_Z^3 + 137\_Z^4$$
$$+ 21\_Z^5 + \_Z^6$$

```
> evalf(sol);
```

$$\{-1.570796327 + 0.8535664710\,I, 1.570796327,$$
$$-0.3257026605, -1.570796327 + 2.473801030\,I,$$
$$0.6948635283, -1.570796327 + 1.767486929\,I,$$
$$-1.570796327 + 3.083849212\,I\}$$

You should check the solution set by plotting the function.

```
> plot( eval(err_xi, x=2), xi=2..4 );
```

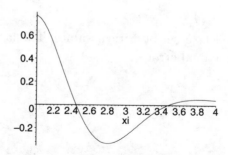

Two solutions to `err_xi=0` seem to exist between 2 and 4 where `solve` found none: $\pi/2$ is less than 2. Thus, you must use numerical methods. If $x = 2$, then ξ should be in the interval from 2 to a.

```
> sol := fsolve( eval(err_xi, x=2), xi, 2..a );
```

$$sol := 2.446729125$$

At that point the error is

```
> eval( err, {x=2, xi=sol});
```

$$0.07333000221 \, (2 - \pi)^6$$

Now add this value to the set of critical values.

```
> critical := critical union {%};
```

$$critical := \{0, \, 0.07333000221 \, (2 - \pi)^6\}$$

If $x = 4$ then ξ should be between a and 4.

```
> sol := fsolve( eval(err_xi, x=4), xi, a..4 );
```

$$sol := 3.467295314$$

At that point, the error is

```
> eval( err, {x=4, xi=sol} );
```

$$-0.01542298119 \left(4 - \pi\right)^6$$

```
> critical := critical union {%};
```

$$critical :=$$
$$\{0, \; -0.01542298119 \left(4 - \pi\right)^6, \; 0.07333000221 \left(2 - \pi\right)^6\}$$

At the $\xi = a$ boundary, the error is

```
> B := eval( err, xi=a );
```

$$B := -\frac{1}{240} \left(x - \pi\right)^6$$

The derivative, $B1$, of B is zero at a critical point.

```
> B1 := diff( B, x );
```

$$B1 := -\frac{1}{40} \left(x - \pi\right)^5$$

```
> sol := { solve( B1=0, x ) };
```

$$sol := \{\pi\}$$

At the critical point the error is

```
> eval( B, x=sol[1] );
```

$$0$$

```
> critical := critical union { % };
```

$$critical :=$$
$$\{0, \; -0.01542298119 \left(4 - \pi\right)^6, \; 0.07333000221 \left(2 - \pi\right)^6\}$$

At the last boundary, $\xi = x$, the error is

```
> B := eval( err, xi=x );
```

$$B := \frac{1}{720}(-\sin(x)\,e^{\sin(x)} + 16\cos(x)^2\,e^{\sin(x)} - 15\sin(x)^2\,e^{\sin(x)}$$
$$+ 75\sin(x)\cos(x)^2\,e^{\sin(x)} - 20\cos(x)^4\,e^{\sin(x)} - 15\sin(x)^3\,e^{\sin(x)}$$
$$+ 45\sin(x)^2\cos(x)^2\,e^{\sin(x)} - 15\sin(x)\cos(x)^4\,e^{\sin(x)}$$
$$+ \cos(x)^6\,e^{\sin(x)})(x - \pi)^6$$

Again, you need to find where the derivative is zero.

```
> B1 := diff( B, x );
```

$$B1 := \frac{1}{720}(-\cos(x)\,e^{\sin(x)} - 63\sin(x)\cos(x)\,e^{\sin(x)}$$
$$+ 91\cos(x)^3\,e^{\sin(x)} - 210\sin(x)^2\cos(x)\,e^{\sin(x)}$$
$$+ 245\sin(x)\cos(x)^3\,e^{\sin(x)} - 35\cos(x)^5\,e^{\sin(x)}$$
$$- 105\sin(x)^3\cos(x)\,e^{\sin(x)} + 105\sin(x)^2\cos(x)^3\,e^{\sin(x)}$$
$$- 21\sin(x)\cos(x)^5\,e^{\sin(x)} + \cos(x)^7\,e^{\sin(x)})(x - \pi)^6 + \frac{1}{120}($$
$$-\sin(x)\,e^{\sin(x)} + 16\cos(x)^2\,e^{\sin(x)} - 15\sin(x)^2\,e^{\sin(x)}$$
$$+ 75\sin(x)\cos(x)^2\,e^{\sin(x)} - 20\cos(x)^4\,e^{\sin(x)} - 15\sin(x)^3\,e^{\sin(x)}$$
$$+ 45\sin(x)^2\cos(x)^2\,e^{\sin(x)} - 15\sin(x)\cos(x)^4\,e^{\sin(x)}$$
$$+ \cos(x)^6\,e^{\sin(x)})(x - \pi)^5$$

```
> sol := { solve( B1=0, x ) };
```

$$sol := \{\pi\}$$

Check the solution by plotting.

```
> plot( B1, x=2..4 );
```

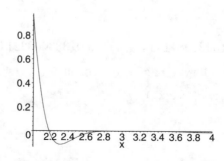

The plot of $B1$ indicates that a solution between 2.1 and 2.3 exists. The **solve** command cannot find that solution, so you must resort to numerical methods again.

```
> fsolve( B1=0, x, 2.1..2.3 );
```

$$2.180293062$$

Add the numerical solution to the set of symbolic solutions.

```
> sol := sol union { % };
```

$$sol := \{2.180293062, \pi\}$$

The following is the set of extremal errors at the $\xi = x$ boundary.

```
> { seq( B, x=sol ) };
```

$$\{0, \, 0.04005698601\,(2.180293062 - \pi)^6\}$$

Now enlarge the set of large errors.

```
> critical := critical union %;
```

$$critical := \{0, \, -0.01542298119\,(4 - \pi)^6,$$
$$0.04005698601\,(2.180293062 - \pi)^6,$$
$$0.07333000221\,(2 - \pi)^6\}$$

Finally, you must add the error at the four corners to the set of critical values.

```
> critical := critical union
>    { eval( err, {xi=2, x=2} ),
>       eval( err, {xi=2, x=4} ),
>       eval( err, {xi=4, x=2} ),
>       eval( err, {xi=4, x=4} ) };
```

$critical := \{0, -0.01542298119\,(4 - \pi)^6,$

$0.04005698601\,(2.180293062 - \pi)^6,$

$0.07333000221\,(2 - \pi)^6, \dfrac{1}{720}(-\sin(2)\,e^{\sin(2)}$

$+ 16\cos(2)^2\,e^{\sin(2)} - 15\sin(2)^2\,e^{\sin(2)} + 75\sin(2)\cos(2)^2\,e^{\sin(2)}$

$- 20\cos(2)^4\,e^{\sin(2)} - 15\sin(2)^3\,e^{\sin(2)}$

$+ 45\sin(2)^2\cos(2)^2\,e^{\sin(2)} - 15\sin(2)\cos(2)^4\,e^{\sin(2)}$

$+ \cos(2)^6\,e^{\sin(2)})(2 - \pi)^6, \dfrac{1}{720}(-\sin(2)\,e^{\sin(2)}$

$+ 16\cos(2)^2\,e^{\sin(2)} - 15\sin(2)^2\,e^{\sin(2)} + 75\sin(2)\cos(2)^2\,e^{\sin(2)}$

$- 20\cos(2)^4\,e^{\sin(2)} - 15\sin(2)^3\,e^{\sin(2)}$

$+ 45\sin(2)^2\cos(2)^2\,e^{\sin(2)} - 15\sin(2)\cos(2)^4\,e^{\sin(2)}$

$+ \cos(2)^6\,e^{\sin(2)})(4 - \pi)^6, \dfrac{1}{720}(-\sin(4)\,e^{\sin(4)}$

$+ 16\cos(4)^2\,e^{\sin(4)} - 15\sin(4)^2\,e^{\sin(4)} + 75\sin(4)\cos(4)^2\,e^{\sin(4)}$

$- 20\cos(4)^4\,e^{\sin(4)} - 15\sin(4)^3\,e^{\sin(4)}$

$+ 45\sin(4)^2\cos(4)^2\,e^{\sin(4)} - 15\sin(4)\cos(4)^4\,e^{\sin(4)}$

$+ \cos(4)^6\,e^{\sin(4)})(2 - \pi)^6, \dfrac{1}{720}(-\sin(4)\,e^{\sin(4)}$

$+ 16\cos(4)^2\,e^{\sin(4)} - 15\sin(4)^2\,e^{\sin(4)} + 75\sin(4)\cos(4)^2\,e^{\sin(4)}$

$- 20\cos(4)^4\,e^{\sin(4)} - 15\sin(4)^3\,e^{\sin(4)}$

$+ 45\sin(4)^2\cos(4)^2\,e^{\sin(4)} - 15\sin(4)\cos(4)^4\,e^{\sin(4)}$

$+ \cos(4)^6\,e^{\sin(4)})(4 - \pi)^6\}$

Now all you need to do is find the maximum of the absolute values of the elements of `critical`. First, map the `abs` command onto the elements of `critical`.

```
> map( abs, critical );
```

$\{0,\ 0.04005698601\,(2.180293062 - \pi)^6,$

$0.07333000221\,(2 - \pi)^6,\ 0.01542298119\,(4 - \pi)^6,\ -\dfrac{1}{720}($

$-\sin(2)\,e^{\sin(2)} + 16\cos(2)^2\,e^{\sin(2)} - 15\sin(2)^2\,e^{\sin(2)}$

$+\,75\sin(2)\cos(2)^2\,e^{\sin(2)} - 20\cos(2)^4\,e^{\sin(2)} - 15\sin(2)^3\,e^{\sin(2)}$

$+\,45\sin(2)^2\cos(2)^2\,e^{\sin(2)} - 15\sin(2)\cos(2)^4\,e^{\sin(2)}$

$+\,\cos(2)^6\,e^{\sin(2)})(2 - \pi)^6,\ -\dfrac{1}{720}(-\sin(2)\,e^{\sin(2)}$

$+\,16\cos(2)^2\,e^{\sin(2)} - 15\sin(2)^2\,e^{\sin(2)} + 75\sin(2)\cos(2)^2\,e^{\sin(2)}$

$-\,20\cos(2)^4\,e^{\sin(2)} - 15\sin(2)^3\,e^{\sin(2)}$

$+\,45\sin(2)^2\cos(2)^2\,e^{\sin(2)} - 15\sin(2)\cos(2)^4\,e^{\sin(2)}$

$+\,\cos(2)^6\,e^{\sin(2)})(4 - \pi)^6,\ -\dfrac{1}{720}(-\sin(4)\,e^{\sin(4)}$

$+\,16\cos(4)^2\,e^{\sin(4)} - 15\sin(4)^2\,e^{\sin(4)} + 75\sin(4)\cos(4)^2\,e^{\sin(4)}$

$-\,20\cos(4)^4\,e^{\sin(4)} - 15\sin(4)^3\,e^{\sin(4)}$

$+\,45\sin(4)^2\cos(4)^2\,e^{\sin(4)} - 15\sin(4)\cos(4)^4\,e^{\sin(4)}$

$+\,\cos(4)^6\,e^{\sin(4)})(2 - \pi)^6,\ -\dfrac{1}{720}(-\sin(4)\,e^{\sin(4)}$

$+\,16\cos(4)^2\,e^{\sin(4)} - 15\sin(4)^2\,e^{\sin(4)} + 75\sin(4)\cos(4)^2\,e^{\sin(4)}$

$-\,20\cos(4)^4\,e^{\sin(4)} - 15\sin(4)^3\,e^{\sin(4)}$

$+\,45\sin(4)^2\cos(4)^2\,e^{\sin(4)} - 15\sin(4)\cos(4)^4\,e^{\sin(4)}$

$+\,\cos(4)^6\,e^{\sin(4)})(4 - \pi)^6\}$

Then find the maximal element. The `max` command expects a sequence of numbers, so you must use the `op` command to convert the set of values into a sequence.

```
> max_error := max( op(%) );
```

$$max\_error := 0.07333000221\,(2 - \pi)^6$$

Approximately, this number is

```
> evalf( max_error );
```

$$0.1623112756$$

You can now plot f, its Taylor approximation, and a pair of curves indicating the error band.

```
> plot( [ f(x), poly, f(x)+max_error, f(x)-max_error ],
>          x=2..4,
>          color=[ red, blue, brown, brown ] );
```

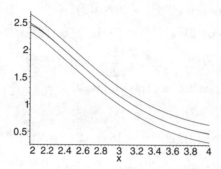

The plot shows that the actual error stays well inside the error estimate.

The Integral

The integral of a function can be considered as a measure of the area between the x-axis and the graph of the function. The definition of the Riemann integral relies on this graphical interpretation of the integral.

```
> f := x ->  1/2 + sin(x);
```

$$f := x \rightarrow \frac{1}{2} + \sin(x)$$

For example, the `ApproximateInt` command with `method = left`, `partition = 6`, and `output = plot` specified, from the `Student[Calculus1]` package draws the graph of f along with 6 boxes. The height of each box is the value of f evaluated at the left-hand side of the box.

```
> with(Student[Calculus1]):


> ApproximateInt( f(x), x=0..10, method=left, partition=6,
>               output=plot);
```

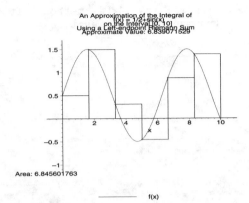

An Approximation of the Integral of
f(x) = 1/2 - sin(x)
on the Interval [0, 10]
Using a Left-endpoint Riemann Sum
Approximate Value: 6.839071529

Area: 6.845601763

———— f(x)

Change output = plot to output = sum to calculate the area of the boxes.

```
> ApproximateInt( f(x), x=0..10, method=left, partition=6,
>          output=sum);
```

$$\frac{5}{3}\left(\sum_{i=0}^{5}\left(\frac{1}{2}+\sin\left(\frac{5}{3}i\right)\right)\right)$$

Approximately, this number is

```
> evalf( % );
```

$$6.845601766$$

The approximation of the area improves as you increase the number of boxes. Increase the number of boxes to 12 and calculate the value of **ApproximateInt** for each of these boxes.

```
> seq( evalf(ApproximateInt( f(x), x=0..10, method=left,
>       partition=n^2)), n=3..14);
```

6.948089404, 6.948819107, 6.923289158, 6.902789479,
6.888196447, 6.877830054, 6.870316620, 6.864739771,
6.860504866, 6.857222010, 6.854630209, 6.852550665

Use the option **output = animation** to create an animation for the left Reimann sum.

```
> ApproximateInt( f(x), x=0..4*Pi, method=left, partition=6,
>                 output=animation, iterations=7);
```

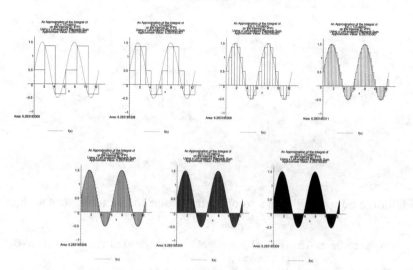

In the limit, as the number of boxes tends to infinity, you obtain the definite integral.

```
> Int( f(x), x=0..10 );
```

$$\int_0^{10} \frac{1}{2} + \sin(x)\, dx$$

The value of the integral is

```
> value( % );
```

$$6 - \cos(10)$$

and in floating-point numbers, this value is approximately

```
> evalf( % );
```

$$6.839071529$$

The indefinite integral of f is

```
> Int( f(x), x );
```

$$\int \frac{1}{2} + \sin(x)\, dx$$

```
> value( % );
```

$$\frac{1}{2}x - \cos(x)$$

Define the function F to be the antiderivative.

```
> F := unapply( %, x );
```

$$F := x \rightarrow \frac{1}{2}x - \cos(x)$$

Choose the constant of integration so that $F(0) = 0$.

```
> F(x) - F(0);
```

$$\frac{1}{2}x - \cos(x) + 1$$

```
> F := unapply( %, x );
```

$$F := x \rightarrow \frac{1}{2}x - \cos(x) + 1$$

If you plot F and the left-boxes together, you can see that F increases more when the corresponding box is larger.

```
> with(plots):
> display( [ plot( F(x), x=0..10, color=blue, legend="F(x)" ),
>            ApproximateInt( f(x), x=0..10, partition=14,
>            method=left, output=plot) ] );
```

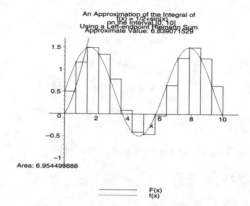

An Approximation of the Integral of
f(x) = 1/2+sin(x)
on the Interval [0, 10]
Using a Left-endpoint Riemann Sum
Approximate Value: 6.838071529

Area: 6.954499888

F(x)
f(x)

By specifying `method = right` or `method = midpoint` when using the `ApproximateInt` command, you can draw and sum boxes evaulated at the right-hand side or at the midpoint of the box.

Mixed Partial Derivatives

This section describes the `D` operator for derivatives and gives an example of a function whose mixed partial derivatives are different.

Consider the following function.

```
> f := (x,y) -> x * y * (x^2-y^2) / (x^2+y^2);
```

$$f := (x,\, y) \to \frac{x\,y\,(x^2 - y^2)}{x^2 + y^2}$$

The function f is not defined at $(0,0)$.

```
> f(0,0);
```

```
Error, (in f) numeric exception: division by zero
```

At $(x, y) = (r\cos(\theta), r\sin(\theta))$ the function value is

```
> f( r*cos(theta), r*sin(theta) );
```

$$\frac{r^2 \cos(\theta)\sin(\theta)\,(r^2\cos(\theta)^2 - r^2\sin(\theta)^2)}{r^2\cos(\theta)^2 + r^2\sin(\theta)^2}$$

As r tends to zero so does the function value.

```
> Limit( %, r=0 );
```

$$\lim_{r \to 0} \frac{r^2 \cos(\theta) \sin(\theta) \left(r^2 \cos(\theta)^2 - r^2 \sin(\theta)^2 \right)}{r^2 \cos(\theta)^2 + r^2 \sin(\theta)^2}$$

```
> value( % );
```

$$0$$

Thus, you can extend f as a continuous function by defining it to be zero at $(0,0)$.

```
> f(0,0) := 0;
```

$$f(0,\, 0) := 0$$

The above assignment places an entry in f's remember table. Here is the graph of f.

```
> plot3d( f, -3..3, -3..3 );
```

The partial derivative of f with respect to its first parameter, x, is

```
> fx := D[1](f);
```

$$fx := (x,\, y) \to \frac{y\,(x^2 - y^2)}{x^2 + y^2} + 2\,\frac{x^2\, y}{x^2 + y^2} - 2\,\frac{x^2\, y\,(x^2 - y^2)}{(x^2 + y^2)^2}$$

This formula does not hold at $(0,0)$.

```
> fx(0,0);
```

```
Error, (in fx) numeric exception: division by zero
```

Therefore, you must use the limit definition of the derivative.

```
> fx(0,0) := limit( ( f(h,0) - f(0,0) )/h, h=0 );
```

$$\text{fx}(0, 0) := 0$$

At $(x, y) = (r\cos(\theta), r\sin(\theta))$ the value of fx is

```
> fx( r*cos(theta), r*sin(theta) );
```

$$\frac{r\sin(\theta)\,(r^2\cos(\theta)^2 - r^2\sin(\theta)^2)}{r^2\cos(\theta)^2 + r^2\sin(\theta)^2} + 2\,\frac{r^3\cos(\theta)^2\sin(\theta)}{r^2\cos(\theta)^2 + r^2\sin(\theta)^2}$$
$$- 2\,\frac{r^3\cos(\theta)^2\sin(\theta)\,(r^2\cos(\theta)^2 - r^2\sin(\theta)^2)}{(r^2\cos(\theta)^2 + r^2\sin(\theta)^2)^2}$$

```
> combine( % );
```

$$\frac{3}{4}r\sin(3\,\theta) - \frac{1}{4}r\sin(5\,\theta)$$

As the distance r from (x, y) to $(0, 0)$ tends to zero, so does $|fx(x, y) - fx(0, 0)|$.

```
> Limit( abs( % - fx(0,0) ), r=0 );
```

$$\lim_{r \to 0} \left| \frac{3}{4}r\sin(3\,\theta) - \frac{1}{4}r\sin(5\,\theta) \right|$$

```
> value( % );
```

$$0$$

Hence, fx is continuous at $(0, 0)$.

By symmetry, the same arguments apply to the derivative of f with respect to its second parameter, y.

```
> fy := D[2](f);
```

$$fy := (x, y) \to \frac{x\,(x^2 - y^2)}{x^2 + y^2} - 2\,\frac{x\,y^2}{x^2 + y^2} - 2\,\frac{x\,y^2\,(x^2 - y^2)}{(x^2 + y^2)^2}$$

```
> fy(0,0) := limit( ( f(0,k) - f(0,0) )/k, k=0 );
```

$$\mathrm{fy}(0,\,0) := 0$$

Here is a mixed second derivative of f.

```
> fxy := D[1,2](f);
```

$$\mathit{fxy} := (x,\,y) \to \frac{x^2 - y^2}{x^2 + y^2} + 2\,\frac{x^2}{x^2 + y^2} - 2\,\frac{x^2\,(x^2 - y^2)}{(x^2 + y^2)^2}$$
$$- 2\,\frac{y^2}{x^2 + y^2} - 2\,\frac{y^2\,(x^2 - y^2)}{(x^2 + y^2)^2} + 8\,\frac{x^2\,y^2\,(x^2 - y^2)}{(x^2 + y^2)^3}$$

Again, the formula does not hold at $(0,0)$.

```
> fxy(0,0);
```

Error, (in fxy) numeric exception: division by zero

The limit definition is

```
> Limit( ( fx(0,k) - fx(0,0) )/k, k=0 );
```

$$\lim_{k \to 0} -1$$

```
> fxy(0,0) := value( % );
```

$$\mathrm{fxy}(0,\,0) := -1$$

The other mixed second derivative is

```
> fyx := D[2,1](f);
```

$$\mathit{fyx} := (x,\,y) \to \frac{x^2 - y^2}{x^2 + y^2} + 2\,\frac{x^2}{x^2 + y^2} - 2\,\frac{x^2\,(x^2 - y^2)}{(x^2 + y^2)^2}$$
$$- 2\,\frac{y^2}{x^2 + y^2} - 2\,\frac{y^2\,(x^2 - y^2)}{(x^2 + y^2)^2} + 8\,\frac{x^2\,y^2\,(x^2 - y^2)}{(x^2 + y^2)^3}$$

At $(0,0)$, you need to use the limit definition.

```
> Limit( ( fy(h, 0) - fy(0,0) )/h, h=0 );
```

$$\lim_{h \to 0} 1$$

```
> fyx(0,0) := value( % );
```

$$\mathrm{fyx}(0, 0) := 1$$

Note that the two mixed partial derivatives are different at $(0,0)$.

```
> fxy(0,0) <> fyx(0,0);
```

$$-1 \neq 1$$

```
> evalb( % );
```

true

The mixed partial derivatives are equal only if they are continuous. If you plot **fxy**, you can see that it is not continuous at $(0,0)$.

```
> plot3d( fxy, -3..3, -3..3 );
```

Maple can help you with many other problems from introductory calculus. For more information, refer to **?Student[Calculus1]**.

6.2   Ordinary Differential Equations

Maple provides you with a varied set of tools for solving, manipulating, and plotting ordinary differential equations and systems of differential equations.

The dsolve Command

The most commonly used command for investigating the behavior of ordinary differential equations (ODEs) in Maple is dsolve. You can use this general-purpose tool to obtain both closed form and numerical solutions to a wide variety of ODEs. This is the basic syntax of dsolve.

```
dsolve(eqns, vars)
```

Here *eqns* is a set of differential equations and initial values, and *vars* is a set of variables with respect to which dsolve solves.

The following example is a differential equation and an initial condition.

```
> eq := diff(v(t),t)+2*t = 0;
```

$$eq := (\frac{d}{dt}\, v(t)) + 2\, t = 0$$

```
> ini := v(1) = 5;
```

$$ini := v(1) = 5$$

Use dsolve to obtain the solution.

```
> dsolve( {eq, ini}, {v(t)} );
```

$$v(t) = -t^2 + 6$$

If you omit some or all of the initial conditions, then dsolve returns a solution containing arbitrary constants of the form _Cnumber.

```
> eq := diff(y(x),x$2) - y(x) = 1;
```

$$eq := (\frac{d^2}{dx^2}\, y(x)) - y(x) = 1$$

```
> dsolve( {eq}, {y(x)} );
```

$$\{y(x) = e^x \_C2 + e^{(-x)} \_C1 - 1\}$$

To specify initial conditions for the derivative of a function, use the following notation.

```
D(fcn)(var_value) = value
(D@@n)(fcn)(var_value) = value
```

The D notation represents the derivative. The D@@n notation represents the *n*th derivative. Here is a differential equation and some initial conditions involving the derivative.

```
> de1 := diff(y(t),t$2) + 5*diff(y(t),t) + 6*y(t) = 0;
```

$$de1 := (\frac{d^2}{dt^2} y(t)) + 5 (\frac{d}{dt} y(t)) + 6 y(t) = 0$$

```
> ini := y(0)=0, D(y)(0)=1;
```

$$ini := y(0) = 0, \, D(y)(0) = 1$$

Again, use dsolve to find the solution.

```
> dsolve( {de1, ini}, {y(t)} );
```

$$y(t) = e^{(-2t)} - e^{(-3t)}$$

Additionally, dsolve may return a solution in parametric form, [x=f(_T), y(x)=g(_T)], where _T is the parameter.

The explicit Option   Maple may return the solution to a differential equation in implicit form.

```
> de2 := diff(y(x),x$2) = (ln(y(x))+1)*diff(y(x),x);
```

$$de2 := \frac{d^2}{dx^2} y(x) = (\ln(y(x)) + 1) (\frac{d}{dx} y(x))$$

```
> dsolve( {de2}, {y(x)} );
```

$$\{\mathrm{y}(x) = \_C1\}, \ \left\{ \int^{y(x)} \frac{1}{\_a \ln(\_a) + \_C1} \, d\_a - x - \_C2 = 0 \right\}$$

Use the `explicit` option to look for an explicit solution for the first result.

```
> dsolve( {de2}, {y(x)}, explicit );
```

$$\{\mathrm{y}(x) = \_C1\},$$
$$\left\{ \mathrm{y}(x) = \mathrm{RootOf} \left(-\int^{-Z} \frac{1}{\_f \ln(\_f) + \_C1} \, d\_f + x + \_C2 \right) \right\}$$

However, in some cases, Maple may not be able to find an explicit solution.

There is also an `implicit` option to force answers to be returned in implicit form.

The `method=laplace` Option Applying Laplace transform methods to differential equations often reduces the complexity of the problem. The transform maps the differential equations into algebraic equations, which are much easier to solve. The difficulty is in the transformation of the equations to the new domain, and especially the transformation of the solutions back.

The Laplace transform method can handle linear ODEs of arbitrary order, and some cases of linear ODEs with non-constant coefficients, provided that Maple can find the transforms. This method can also solve systems of coupled equations.

Consider the following problem in classical dynamics. Two weights with masses m and αm, respectively, rest on a frictionless plane joined by a spring with spring constant k. What are the trajectories of each weight if the first weight is subject to a unit step force $u(t)$ at time $t = 1$? First, set up the differential equations that govern the system. Newton's Second Law governs the motion of the first weight, and hence, the mass m times the acceleration must equal the sum of the forces that you apply to the first weight, including the external force $u(t)$.

```
> eqn1 :=
>   alpha*m*diff(x[1](t),t$2) = k*(x[2](t) - x[1](t)) + u(t);
```

$$eqn1 := \alpha\, m\, (\frac{d^2}{dt^2}\, x_1(t)) = k\, (x_2(t) - x_1(t)) + \mathrm{u}(t)$$

Similarly for the second weight.

```
> eqn2 := m*diff(x[2](t),t$2) = k*(x[1](t) - x[2](t));
```

$$eqn2 := m\, (\frac{d^2}{dt^2}\, x_2(t)) = k\, (x_1(t) - x_2(t))$$

Apply a unit step force to the first weight at $t = 1$.

```
> u := t -> Heaviside(t-1);
```

$$u := t \rightarrow \mathrm{Heaviside}(t - 1)$$

At time $t = 0$, both masses are at rest at their respective locations.

```
> ini := x[1](0) = 2, D(x[1])(0) = 0,
>          x[2](0) = 0, D(x[2])(0) = 0 ;
```

$$ini := x_1(0) = 2,\, \mathrm{D}(x_1)(0) = 0,\, x_2(0) = 0,\, \mathrm{D}(x_2)(0) = 0$$

Solve the problem using Laplace transform methods.

```
> dsolve( {eqn1, eqn2, ini}, {x[1](t), x[2](t)},
>    method=laplace );
```

$$\left\{ x_2(t) = \frac{1}{2}(t^2 \, k \, \alpha + \alpha \, k - 2 \, t \, k \, \alpha - 2 \, \alpha \, m \right.$$

$$+ 2 \, \alpha \cosh(\frac{\sqrt{\%1} \, (t-1)}{\alpha \, m}) \, m + t^2 \, k + k - 2 \, t \, k)$$

$$\text{Heaviside}(t-1) \, \Big/ ((1 + 2 \, \alpha + \alpha^2) \, k \, m)$$

$$- 2 \, \frac{\alpha \, (-1 + \cosh(\frac{\sqrt{\%1} \, t}{\alpha \, m}))}{1 + \alpha}, x_1(t) =$$

$$- \frac{\text{Heaviside}(t-1) \cosh(\frac{\sqrt{\%1} \, (t-1)}{\alpha \, m})}{k \, (1 + \alpha)^2}$$

$$- 2 \, \frac{\alpha \cosh(\frac{\sqrt{\%1} \, t}{\alpha \, m})}{1 + \alpha} + e^{(-\frac{\sqrt{\%1} \, t}{\alpha \, m})} + e^{(\frac{\sqrt{\%1} \, t}{\alpha \, m})} + ($$

$$\frac{1}{2} \, k \, \text{Heaviside}(t-1) \, (1 + \alpha) \, t^2$$

$$- k \, \text{Heaviside}(t-1) \, (1 + \alpha) \, t + 2 \, \alpha^2 \, m \, k$$

$$+ \text{Heaviside}(t-1) \, m + \frac{1}{2} \, \text{Heaviside}(t-1) \, \alpha \, k$$

$$\left. + 2 \, \alpha \, m \, k + \frac{1}{2} \, \text{Heaviside}(t-1) \, k) \, \Big/ ((1 + \alpha)^2 \, k \, m) \right\}$$

$$\%1 := -\alpha \, m \, k \, (1 + \alpha)$$

Evaluate the result at values for the constants.

```
> ans := eval( %, {alpha=1/10, m=1, k=1} );
```

$$ans := \{x_2(t) = \frac{50}{121}$$

$$(\frac{11}{10}t^2 + \frac{9}{10} - \frac{11}{5}t + \frac{1}{5}\cosh(\frac{1}{10}\sqrt{-11}\sqrt{100}\,(t-1)))$$

$$\text{Heaviside}(t-1) + \frac{2}{11} - \frac{2}{11}\cosh(\frac{1}{10}\sqrt{-11}\sqrt{100}\,t), x_1(t)$$

$$= -\frac{100}{121}\text{Heaviside}(t-1)\cosh(\frac{1}{10}\sqrt{-11}\sqrt{100}\,(t-1))$$

$$- \frac{2}{11}\cosh(\frac{1}{10}\sqrt{-11}\sqrt{100}\,t) + e^{(-1/10\sqrt{-11}\sqrt{100}\,t)}$$

$$+ e^{(1/10\sqrt{-11}\sqrt{100}\,t)} + \frac{5}{11}\text{Heaviside}(t-1)\,t^2$$

$$- \frac{10}{11}\text{Heaviside}(t-1)\,t + \frac{2}{11} + \frac{155}{121}\text{Heaviside}(t-1)\}$$

You can turn the above solution into two functions, say $y_1(t)$ and $y_2(t)$, as follows. First evaluate the expression x[1](t) at the solution to select the $x_1(t)$ expression.

```
> eval( x[1](t), ans );
```

$$-\frac{100}{121}\text{Heaviside}(t-1)\cosh(\frac{1}{10}\sqrt{-11}\sqrt{100}\,(t-1))$$

$$- \frac{2}{11}\cosh(\frac{1}{10}\sqrt{-11}\sqrt{100}\,t) + e^{(-1/10\sqrt{-11}\sqrt{100}\,t)}$$

$$+ e^{(1/10\sqrt{-11}\sqrt{100}\,t)} + \frac{5}{11}\text{Heaviside}(t-1)\,t^2$$

$$- \frac{10}{11}\text{Heaviside}(t-1)\,t + \frac{2}{11} + \frac{155}{121}\text{Heaviside}(t-1)$$

Then convert the expression to a function by using **unapply**.

```
> y[1] := unapply( %, t );
```

$$y_1 := t \rightarrow$$

$$-\frac{100}{121}\text{Heaviside}(t-1)\cosh(\frac{1}{10}\sqrt{-11}\sqrt{100}\,(t-1))$$

$$- \frac{2}{11}\cosh(\frac{1}{10}\sqrt{-11}\sqrt{100}\,t) + e^{(-1/10\sqrt{-11}\sqrt{100}\,t)}$$

$$+ e^{(1/10\sqrt{-11}\sqrt{100}\,t)} + \frac{5}{11}\text{Heaviside}(t-1)\,t^2$$

$$- \frac{10}{11}\text{Heaviside}(t-1)\,t + \frac{2}{11} + \frac{155}{121}\text{Heaviside}(t-1)$$

You can also do the two steps at once.

```
> y[2] := unapply( eval( x[2](t), ans ), t );
```

$$y_2 := t \to \frac{50}{121}$$
$$(\frac{11}{10} t^2 + \frac{9}{10} - \frac{11}{5} t + \frac{1}{5} \cosh(\frac{1}{10} \sqrt{-11} \sqrt{100} (t-1)))$$
$$\text{Heaviside}(t-1) + \frac{2}{11} - \frac{2}{11} \cosh(\frac{1}{10} \sqrt{-11} \sqrt{100} t)$$

Now plot the two functions.

```
> plot( [ y[1](t), y[2](t) ], t=-3..6 );
```

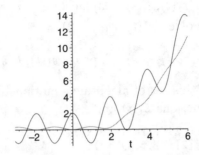

Instead of using `dsolve(..., method=laplace)`, you can use the Laplace transform method by hand. The `inttrans` package defines the Laplace transform and its inverse (and many other integral transforms).

```
> with(inttrans);
```

[*addtable, fourier, fouriercos, fouriersin, hankel, hilbert,*
invfourier, invhilbert, invlaplace, invmellin, laplace,
mellin, savetable]

The Laplace transforms of the two differential equations `eqn1` and `eqn2` are

```
> laplace( eqn1, t, s );
```

$$\alpha m \left(s \left(s \, \text{laplace}(x_1(t), t, s) - x_1(0)\right) - D(x_1)(0)\right) =$$
$$k \left(\text{laplace}(x_2(t), t, s) - \text{laplace}(x_1(t), t, s)\right) + \frac{e^{(-s)}}{s}$$

and

```
> laplace( eqn2, t, s );
```

$$m\left(s\left(s\,\mathrm{laplace}(x_2(t),\ t,\ s)\right) - x_2(0)\right) - D(x_2)(0)) =$$
$$k\left(\mathrm{laplace}(x_1(t),\ t,\ s) - \mathrm{laplace}(x_2(t),\ t,\ s)\right)$$

Evaluate the set consisting of the two transforms at the initial conditions.

```
> eval( {%, %%}, {ini} );
```

$$\{m\,s^2\,\mathrm{laplace}(x_2(t),\ t,\ s) =$$
$$k\left(\mathrm{laplace}(x_1(t),\ t,\ s) - \mathrm{laplace}(x_2(t),\ t,\ s)\right),$$
$$\alpha\,m\,s\left(s\,\mathrm{laplace}(x_1(t),\ t,\ s) - 2\right) =$$
$$k\left(\mathrm{laplace}(x_2(t),\ t,\ s) - \mathrm{laplace}(x_1(t),\ t,\ s)\right) + \frac{e^{(-s)}}{s}\}$$

You must solve this set of algebraic equations for the Laplace transforms of the two functions $x_1(t)$ and $x_2(t)$.

```
> sol := solve( %, { laplace(x[1](t),t,s),
>    laplace(x[2](t),t,s) } );
```

$$sol := \{\mathrm{laplace}(x_1(t),\ t,\ s) = \frac{(m\,s^2 + k)\,(2\,\alpha\,m\,s^2\,e^s + 1)}{e^s\,s^3\,m\,(k + \alpha\,m\,s^2 + \alpha\,k)},$$
$$\mathrm{laplace}(x_2(t),\ t,\ s) = \frac{k\,(2\,\alpha\,m\,s^2\,e^s + 1)}{e^s\,s^3\,m\,(k + \alpha\,m\,s^2 + \alpha\,k)}\}$$

Maple has solved the algebraic problem. You must take the inverse Laplace transform to get the functions $x_1(t)$ and $x_2(t)$.

```
> invlaplace( %, s, t );
```

$$\left\{ x_2(t) = k \left(\frac{1}{2}(t^2\,k\,\alpha + \alpha\,k - 2\,t\,k\,\alpha - 2\,\alpha\,m \right.\right.$$

$$+ 2\,\alpha \cosh(\frac{\sqrt{\%1}\,(t-1)}{\alpha\,m})\,m + t^2\,k + k - 2\,t\,k)$$

$$\text{Heaviside}(t-1) \Big/ ((1+\alpha)^2\,k^2)$$

$$\left. -2\,\frac{\alpha\,m\,(-1+\cosh(\frac{\sqrt{\%1}\,t}{\alpha\,m}))}{k\,(1+\alpha)} \right) \Big/ m, x_1(t) =$$

$$-\frac{\text{Heaviside}(t-1)\cosh(\frac{\sqrt{\%1}\,(t-1)}{\alpha\,m})}{k\,(1+\alpha)^2}$$

$$-2\,\frac{\alpha \cosh(\frac{\sqrt{\%1}\,t}{\alpha\,m})}{1+\alpha} + e^{(-\frac{\sqrt{\%1}\,t}{\alpha\,m})} + e^{(\frac{\sqrt{\%1}\,t}{\alpha\,m})} + ($$

$$\frac{1}{2}\,k\,\text{Heaviside}(t-1)\,(1+\alpha)\,t^2$$

$$- k\,\text{Heaviside}(t-1)\,(1+\alpha)\,t + 2\,\alpha^2\,m\,k$$

$$+ \text{Heaviside}(t-1)\,m + \frac{1}{2}\,\text{Heaviside}(t-1)\,\alpha\,k$$

$$\left. + 2\,\alpha\,m\,k + \frac{1}{2}\,\text{Heaviside}(t-1)\,k) \Big/ ((1+\alpha)^2\,k\,m) \right\}$$

$$\%1 := -\alpha\,m\,k\,(1+\alpha)$$

Evaluate at values for the constants.

```
> eval( %, {alpha=1/10, m=1, k=1} );
```

$$\{x_2(t) = \frac{50}{121}$$

$$(\frac{11}{10}\,t^2 + \frac{9}{10} - \frac{11}{5}\,t + \frac{1}{5}\cosh(\frac{1}{10}\,\sqrt{-11}\,\sqrt{100}\,(t-1)))$$

$$\text{Heaviside}(t-1) + \frac{2}{11} - \frac{2}{11}\cosh(\frac{1}{10}\,\sqrt{-11}\,\sqrt{100}\,t), x_1(t)$$

$$= -\frac{100}{121}\,\text{Heaviside}(t-1)\cosh(\frac{1}{10}\,\sqrt{-11}\,\sqrt{100}\,(t-1))$$

$$-\frac{2}{11}\cosh(\frac{1}{10}\,\sqrt{-11}\,\sqrt{100}\,t) + e^{(-1/10\,\sqrt{-11}\,\sqrt{100}\,t)}$$

$$+ e^{(1/10\,\sqrt{-11}\,\sqrt{100}\,t)} + \frac{5}{11}\,\text{Heaviside}(t-1)\,t^2$$

$$-\frac{10}{11}\,\text{Heaviside}(t-1)\,t + \frac{2}{11} + \frac{155}{121}\,\text{Heaviside}(t-1)\}$$

As expected, you get the same solution as before.

The `type=series` Option The series method for solving differential equations finds an approximate symbolic solution to the equations in the following manner. Maple finds a series approximation to the equations. It then solves the series approximation symbolically, using exact methods. This technique is useful when Maple's standard algorithms fail, but you still want a symbolic solution rather than a purely numeric solution. The series method can often help with nonlinear and high-order ODEs.

When using the series method, Maple assumes that a solution of the form

$$x^c\left(\sum_{i=0}^{\infty} a_i x^i\right)$$

exists, where c is a rational number.

Consider the following differential equation.

```
> eq := 2*x*diff(y(x),x,x) + diff(y(x),x) + y(x) = 0;
```

$$eq := 2\,x\,(\frac{d^2}{dx^2}\,y(x)) + (\frac{d}{dx}\,y(x)) + y(x) = 0$$

Solve the equation.

```
> dsolve( {eq}, {y(x)}, type=series );
```

$$y(x) = \_C1\ \sqrt{x}(1 - \frac{1}{3}\,x + \frac{1}{30}\,x^2 - \frac{1}{630}\,x^3 + \frac{1}{22680}\,x^4 -$$

$$\frac{1}{1247400}\,x^5 + O(x^6)) + \_C2$$

$$(1 - x + \frac{1}{6}\,x^2 - \frac{1}{90}\,x^3 + \frac{1}{2520}\,x^4 - \frac{1}{113400}\,x^5 + O(x^6))$$

Use **rhs** to select the solution, then convert it to a polynomial.

```
> rhs(%);
```

$$\_C1\ \sqrt{x}(1 - \frac{1}{3}\,x + \frac{1}{30}\,x^2 - \frac{1}{630}\,x^3 + \frac{1}{22680}\,x^4 - \frac{1}{1247400}$$

$$x^5 + O(x^6)) + \_C2$$

$$(1 - x + \frac{1}{6}\,x^2 - \frac{1}{90}\,x^3 + \frac{1}{2520}\,x^4 - \frac{1}{113400}\,x^5 + O(x^6))$$

```
> poly := convert(%, polynom);
```

$$poly := \_C1\ \sqrt{x}$$

$$(1 - \frac{1}{3}\,x + \frac{1}{30}\,x^2 - \frac{1}{630}\,x^3 + \frac{1}{22680}\,x^4 - \frac{1}{1247400}\,x^5)$$

$$+ \_C2\ (1 - x + \frac{1}{6}\,x^2 - \frac{1}{90}\,x^3 + \frac{1}{2520}\,x^4 - \frac{1}{113400}\,x^5)$$

Now you can plot the solution for different values of the arbitrary constants _C1 and _C2.

```
> [ seq( _C1=i, i=0..5 ) ];
```

$$[\_C1 = 0,\ \_C1 = 1,\ \_C1 = 2,\ \_C1 = 3,\ \_C1 = 4,\ \_C1 = 5]$$

```
> map(subs, %, _C2=1, poly);
```

$$[1 - x + \frac{1}{6}x^2 - \frac{1}{90}x^3 + \frac{1}{2520}x^4 - \frac{1}{113400}x^5,$$

$$\%1 + 1 - x + \frac{1}{6}x^2 - \frac{1}{90}x^3 + \frac{1}{2520}x^4 - \frac{1}{113400}x^5,$$

$$2\%1 + 1 - x + \frac{1}{6}x^2 - \frac{1}{90}x^3 + \frac{1}{2520}x^4 - \frac{1}{113400}x^5,$$

$$3\%1 + 1 - x + \frac{1}{6}x^2 - \frac{1}{90}x^3 + \frac{1}{2520}x^4 - \frac{1}{113400}x^5,$$

$$4\%1 + 1 - x + \frac{1}{6}x^2 - \frac{1}{90}x^3 + \frac{1}{2520}x^4 - \frac{1}{113400}x^5,$$

$$5\%1 + 1 - x + \frac{1}{6}x^2 - \frac{1}{90}x^3 + \frac{1}{2520}x^4 - \frac{1}{113400}x^5]$$

$$\%1 :=$$

$$\sqrt{x}\left(1 - \frac{1}{3}x + \frac{1}{30}x^2 - \frac{1}{630}x^3 + \frac{1}{22680}x^4 - \frac{1}{1247400}x^5\right)$$

```
> plot( %, x=1..10 );
```

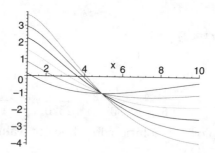

The `type=numeric` **Option** Although the series methods for solving ODEs are well understood and adequate for finding accurate approximations of the dependent variable, they do exhibit some limitations. To obtain a result, the resultant series must converge. Moreover, in the process of finding the solution, Maple must calculate many derivatives, which can be expensive in terms of time and memory. For these and other reasons, alternative numerical solvers have been developed.

Here is a differential equation and an initial condition.

```
> eq := x(t) * diff(x(t), t) = t^2;
```

$$eq := x(t)\left(\frac{d}{dt}x(t)\right) = t^2$$

```
> ini := x(1) = 2;
```

$$ini := \mathrm{x}(1) = 2$$

The output from the `dsolve` command with the `numeric` option is a procedure that returns a list of equations.

```
> sol := dsolve( {eq, ini}, {x(t)}, type=numeric );
```

$$sol := \mathbf{proc}(x\_rkf45) \dots \mathbf{end\ proc}$$

The solution satisfies the initial condition.

```
> sol(1);
```

$$[t = 1., \mathrm{x}(t) = 2.]$$

```
> sol(0);
```

$$[t = 0., \mathrm{x}(t) = 1.82574790049820024]$$

Use the `eval` command to select a particular value from the list of equations.

```
> eval( x(t), sol(1) );
```

$$2.$$

You can also create an ordered pair.

```
> eval( [t, x(t)], sol(0) );
```

$$[0., 1.82574790049820024]$$

The `plots` package contains a command, `odeplot`, for plotting the result of `dsolve( ..., type=numeric)`.

```
> with(plots):
```

```
> odeplot( sol, [t, x(t)], -1..2 );
```

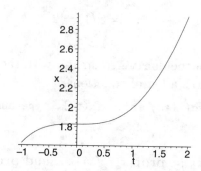

For the syntax of **odeplot**, refer to **?plots,odeplot**.
Here is a system of two ODEs.

```
> eq1 := diff(x(t),t) = y(t);
```

$$eq1 := \frac{d}{dt} x(t) = y(t)$$

```
> eq2 := diff(y(t),t) = x(t)+y(t);
```

$$eq2 := \frac{d}{dt} y(t) = x(t) + y(t)$$

```
> ini :=  x(0)=2, y(0)=1;
```

$$ini := x(0) = 2, \; y(0) = 1$$

In this case, the solution-procedure yields a list of three equations.

```
> sol1 := dsolve( {eq1, eq2, ini}, {x(t),y(t)},
>     type=numeric );
```

$$sol1 := \mathbf{proc}(x\_rkf45) \; \ldots \; \mathbf{end \; proc}$$

```
> sol1(0);
```

$$[t = 0., \; x(t) = 2., \; y(t) = 1.]$$

```
> sol1(1);
```

$$[t = 1., \mathrm{x}(t) = 5.58216755967155986,$$
$$\mathrm{y}(t) = 7.82688931187210190]$$

Use the `odeplot` command to plot `y(t)` against `x(t)`,

```
> odeplot( sol1, [x(t), y(t)], -3..1, labels=["x","y"] );
```

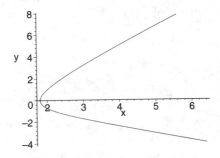

`x(t)` and `y(t)` against `t`,

```
> odeplot( sol1, [t, x(t), y(t)], -3..1,
>    labels=["t","x","y"], axes=boxed );
```

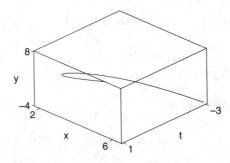

or any other combination.

Always use caution when using numeric methods because errors can accumulate in floating-point calculations. Universal rules for preventing this effect do not exist, so no software package can anticipate all conditions. The solution is to use the `startinit` option to make `dsolve` (or rather the procedure which `dsolve` returns) begin at the initial value for every calculation at a point $(x, y(x))$.

You can specify which algorithm `dsolve(..., type=numeric)` uses when solving your differential equation. Refer to `?dsolve,numeric`.

Example: Taylor Series

In its general form, a series method solution to an ODE requires the forming of a Taylor series about $t = 0$ for some function $f(t)$. Thus, you must be able to obtain and manipulate the higher order derivatives of your function, $f'(t)$, $f''(t)$, $f'''(t)$, and so on.

Once you have obtained the derivatives, you substitute them into the Taylor series representation of $f(t)$.

```
> taylor(f(t), t);
```

$$f(0) + \mathrm{D}(f)(0)\, t + \frac{1}{2}\, (\mathrm{D}^{(2)})(f)(0)\, t^2 + \frac{1}{6}\, (\mathrm{D}^{(3)})(f)(0)\, t^3 +$$
$$\frac{1}{24}\, (\mathrm{D}^{(4)})(f)(0)\, t^4 + \frac{1}{120}\, (\mathrm{D}^{(5)})(f)(0)\, t^5 + \mathrm{O}(t^6)$$

As an example, consider Newton's Law of Cooling:

$$\frac{d\theta}{dt} = -\frac{1}{10}(\theta - 20), \qquad \theta(0) = 100.$$

Using the D operator, you can easily enter the above equation into Maple.

```
> eq := D(theta) = -1/10*(theta-20);
```

$$eq := \mathrm{D}(\theta) = -\frac{1}{10}\,\theta + 2$$

```
> ini := theta(0)=100;
```

$$ini := \theta(0) = 100$$

The first step is to obtain the required number of higher derivatives. Determine this number from the order of your Taylor series. If you use the default value of Order that Maple provides,

```
> Order;
```

$$6$$

then you must generate derivatives up to order

```
> dev_order := Order - 1;
```

$$dev\_order := 5$$

You can now use **seq** to generate a sequence of the higher order derivatives of **theta(t)**.

```
> S := seq( (D@@(dev_order-n))(eq), n=1..dev_order );
```

$$S := (\mathrm{D}^{(5)})(\theta) = -\frac{1}{10}(\mathrm{D}^{(4)})(\theta),\ (\mathrm{D}^{(4)})(\theta) = -\frac{1}{10}(\mathrm{D}^{(3)})(\theta),$$

$$(\mathrm{D}^{(3)})(\theta) = -\frac{1}{10}(\mathrm{D}^{(2)})(\theta),\ (\mathrm{D}^{(2)})(\theta) = -\frac{1}{10}\mathrm{D}(\theta),$$

$$\mathrm{D}(\theta) = -\frac{1}{10}\theta + 2$$

The fifth derivative is a function of the fourth derivative, the fourth a function of the third and so on. Therefore, if you make substitutions according to S, you can express all the derivatives as functions of **theta**. For example, the third element of S is the following.

```
> S[3];
```

$$(\mathrm{D}^{(3)})(\theta) = -\frac{1}{10}(\mathrm{D}^{(2)})(\theta)$$

Substituting according to S on the right-hand side, yields

```
> lhs(%) = subs( S, rhs(%) );
```

$$(\mathrm{D}^{(3)})(\theta) = -\frac{1}{1000}\theta + \frac{1}{50}$$

To make this substitution on all the derivatives at once, use the **map** command.

```
> L := map( z -> lhs(z) = eval(rhs(z), {S}), [S] );
```

$$L := [(\mathrm{D}^{(5)})(\theta) = \frac{1}{100}(\mathrm{D}^{(3)})(\theta),\ (\mathrm{D}^{(4)})(\theta) = \frac{1}{100}(\mathrm{D}^{(2)})(\theta),$$

$$(\mathrm{D}^{(3)})(\theta) = \frac{1}{100}\mathrm{D}(\theta),\ (\mathrm{D}^{(2)})(\theta) = \frac{1}{100}\theta - \frac{1}{5},$$

$$\mathrm{D}(\theta) = -\frac{1}{10}\theta + 2]$$

You must evaluate the derivatives at $t = 0$.

```
> L(0);
```

$$[(D^{(5)})(\theta)(0) = \frac{1}{100} (D^{(3)})(\theta)(0),$$

$$(D^{(4)})(\theta)(0) = \frac{1}{100} (D^{(2)})(\theta)(0),$$

$$(D^{(3)})(\theta)(0) = \frac{1}{100} D(\theta)(0), (D^{(2)})(\theta)(0) = \frac{1}{100} \theta(0) - \frac{1}{5},$$

$$D(\theta)(0) = -\frac{1}{10} \theta(0) + 2]$$

Now generate the Taylor series.

```
> T := taylor(theta(t), t);
```

$$T := \theta(0) + D(\theta)(0) t + \frac{1}{2} (D^{(2)})(\theta)(0) t^2 + \frac{1}{6} (D^{(3)})(\theta)(0)$$

$$t^3 + \frac{1}{24} (D^{(4)})(\theta)(0) t^4 + \frac{1}{120} (D^{(5)})(\theta)(0) t^5 + O(t^6)$$

Substitute the derivatives into the series.

```
> subs( op(L(0)), T );
```

$$\theta(0) + (-\frac{1}{10} \theta(0) + 2) t + (\frac{1}{200} \theta(0) - \frac{1}{10}) t^2 +$$

$$(-\frac{1}{6000} \theta(0) + \frac{1}{300}) t^3 + (\frac{1}{240000} \theta(0) - \frac{1}{12000}) t^4 +$$

$$(-\frac{1}{12000000} \theta(0) + \frac{1}{600000}) t^5 + O(t^6)$$

Now, evaluate the series at the initial condition and convert it to a polynomial.

```
> eval( %, ini );
```

$$100 - 8t + \frac{2}{5} t^2 - \frac{1}{75} t^3 + \frac{1}{3000} t^4 - \frac{1}{150000} t^5 + O(t^6)$$

```
> p := convert(%, polynom);
```

$$p := 100 - 8t + \frac{2}{5} t^2 - \frac{1}{75} t^3 + \frac{1}{3000} t^4 - \frac{1}{150000} t^5$$

You can now plot the response.

```
> plot(p, t=0..30);
```

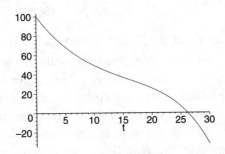

This particular example has the following analytic solution.

```
> dsolve( {eq(t), ini}, {theta(t)} );
```

$$\theta(t) = 20 + 80\,e^{(-1/10\,t)}$$

```
> q := rhs(%);
```

$$q := 20 + 80\,e^{(-1/10\,t)}$$

Thus, you can compare the series solution with the actual solution.

```
> plot( [p, q], t=0..30 );
```

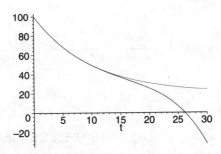

Instead of finding the Taylor series by hand, you can use the **series** option of the **dsolve** command.

```
> dsolve( {eq(t), ini}, {theta(t)}, 'series' );
```

$$\theta(t) =$$

$$100 - 8t + \frac{2}{5}t^2 - \frac{1}{75}t^3 + \frac{1}{3000}t^4 - \frac{1}{150000}t^5 + O(t^6)$$

When You Cannot Find a Closed Form Solution

In some instances, you cannot express the solution to a linear ODE in closed form. In such cases, `dsolve` may return solutions containing the data structure DESol. DESol is a place holder representing the solution of a differential equation without explicitly computing it. Thus, DESol is similar to `RootOf`, which represents the roots of an expression. This allows you to manipulate the resulting expression symbolically prior to attempting another approach.

```
> de := (x^7+x^3-3)*diff(y(x),x,x) + x^4*diff(y(x),x)
>        + (23*x-17)*y(x);
```

$$de :=$$
$$(x^7 + x^3 - 3)\left(\frac{d^2}{dx^2}\,y(x)\right) + x^4\left(\frac{d}{dx}\,y(x)\right) + (23\,x - 17)\,y(x)$$

The `dsolve` command cannot find a closed form solution to `de`.

```
> dsolve( de, y(x) );
```

$$y(x) = \text{DESol}\left($$

$$\left\{\left(\frac{d^2}{dx^2}\,\_Y(x)\right) + \frac{x^4\left(\frac{d}{dx}\,\_Y(x)\right)}{x^7 + x^3 - 3} + \frac{(23\,x - 17)\,\_Y(x)}{x^7 + x^3 - 3}\right\},$$

$$\{\_Y(x)\}\right)$$

You can now try another method on the DESol itself. For example, find a series approximation.

```
> series(rhs(%), x);
```

$$\_Y(0) + \mathrm{D}(\_Y)(0)\,x - \frac{17}{6}\,\_Y(0)\,x^2 +$$

$$\left(-\frac{17}{18}\,\mathrm{D}(\_Y)(0) + \frac{23}{18}\,\_Y(0)\right) x^3 +$$

$$\left(\frac{289}{216}\,\_Y(0) + \frac{23}{36}\,\mathrm{D}(\_Y)(0)\right) x^4 +$$

$$\left(\frac{289}{1080}\,\mathrm{D}(\_Y)(0) - \frac{833}{540}\,\_Y(0)\right) x^5 + \mathrm{O}(x^6)$$

The `diff` and `int` commands can also operate on `DESol`.

Plotting Ordinary Differential Equations

You cannot solve many differential equations analytically. In such cases, plotting the differential equation is advantageous.

```
> ode1 :=
> diff(y(t), t$2) + sin(t)^2*diff(y(t),t) + y(t) = cos(t)^2;
```

$$ode1 := \left(\frac{d^2}{dt^2}\,y(t)\right) + \sin(t)^2\left(\frac{d}{dt}\,y(t)\right) + y(t) = \cos(t)^2$$

```
> ic1 := y(0) = 1, D(y)(0) = 0;
```

$$ic1 := y(0) = 1, \ \mathrm{D}(y)(0) = 0$$

First, attempt to solve this ODE analytically by using `dsolve`.

```
> dsolve({ode1, ic1}, {y(t)} );
```

The `dsolve` command returned nothing, indicating that it could not find a solution. Try Laplace methods.

```
> dsolve( {ode1, ic1}, {y(t)}, method=laplace );
```

Again, `dsolve` did not find a solution. Since `dsolve` was not successful, try the `DEplot` command found in the `DEtools` package.

```
> with(DEtools):
```

`DEplot` is a general ODE plotter which you can use with the following syntax.

```
DEplot( ode, dep-var, range, [ini-conds] )
```

Here *ode* is the differential equation you want to plot, *dep-var* is the dependent variable, *range* is the range of the independent variable, and *ini-conds* is a list of initial conditions.

Here is a plot of the function satisfying both the differential equation **ode1** and the initial conditions **ic1** above.

```
> DEplot( ode1, y(t), 0..20, [ [ ic1 ] ] );
```

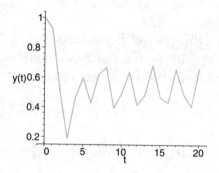

You can refine the plot by specifying a smaller **stepsize**.

```
> DEplot( ode1, y(t), 0..20, [ [ ic1 ] ], stepsize=0.2 );
```

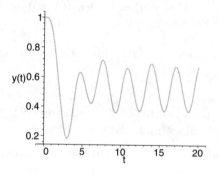

If you specify more than one list of initial conditions, **DEplot** plots a solution for each.

```
> ic2 := y(0)=0, D(y)(0)=1;
```

$$ic2 := y(0) = 0, \mathrm{D}(y)(0) = 1$$

```
> DEplot( ode1, y(t), 0..20, [ [ic1], [ic2] ], stepsize=0.2 );
```

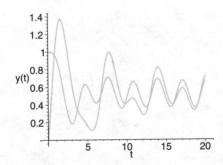

DEplot can also plot solutions to a set of differential equations.

```
> eq1 := diff(y(t),t) + y(t) + x(t) = 0;
```

$$eq1 := (\frac{d}{dt}\,y(t)) + y(t) + x(t) = 0$$

```
> eq2 := y(t) = diff(x(t), t);
```

$$eq2 := y(t) = \frac{d}{dt}\,x(t)$$

```
> ini1 := x(0)=0, y(0)=5;
```

$$ini1 := x(0) = 0,\, y(0) = 5$$

```
> ini2 := x(0)=0, y(0)=-5;
```

$$ini2 := x(0) = 0,\, y(0) = -5$$

The system {eq1, eq2} has two dependent variables, x(t) and y(t), so you must include a list of dependent variables.

```
> DEplot( {eq1, eq2}, [x(t), y(t)], -5..5,
> [ [ini1], [ini2] ] );
```

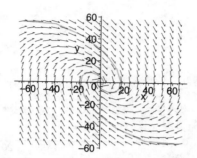

Note that **DEplot** also generates a direction field, as above, whenever it is meaningful to do so. For more details on how to plot ODEs, refer to ?DEtools,DEplot.

DEplot3d is the three-dimensional version of **DEplot**. The basic syntax of **DEplot3d** is similar to that of **DEplot**. For details, refer to ?DEtools,DEplot3d. The following is a three-dimensional plot of the system plotted in two dimensions above.

```
> DEplot3d( {eq1, eq2}, [x(t), y(t)], -5..5,
> [ [ini1], [ini2] ] );
```

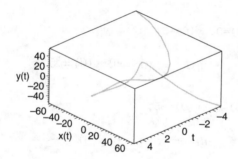

The following is an example of a plot of a system of three differential equations.

```
> eq1 := diff(x(t),t) = y(t)+z(t);
```

$$eq1 := \frac{d}{dt}\,\mathrm{x}(t) = \mathrm{y}(t) + \mathrm{z}(t)$$

```
> eq2 := diff(y(t),t) = -x(t)-y(t);
```

$$eq2 := \frac{d}{dt}\,y(t) = -y(t) - x(t)$$

```
> eq3 := diff(z(t),t) = x(t)+y(t)-z(t);
```

$$eq3 := \frac{d}{dt}\,z(t) = x(t) + y(t) - z(t)$$

These are two lists of initial conditions.

```
> ini1 := [x(0)=1, y(0)=0, z(0)=2];
```

$$ini1 := [x(0) = 1,\ y(0) = 0,\ z(0) = 2]$$

```
> ini2 := [x(0)=0, y(0)=2, z(0)=-1];
```

$$ini2 := [x(0) = 0,\ y(0) = 2,\ z(0) = -1]$$

The `DEplot3d` command plots two solutions to the system of differential equations {`eq1`, `eq2`, `eq3`}, one solution for each list of initial values.

```
> DEplot3d( {eq1, eq2, eq3}, [x(t), y(t), z(t)], t=0..10,
>      [ini1, ini2], stepsize=0.1, orientation=[-171, 58] );
```

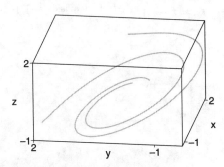

Discontinuous Forcing Functions

In many practical instances the forcing function to a system is discontinuous. Maple provides a number of ways in which you can describe a system in terms of ODEs and include, in a meaningful way, descriptions of discontinuous forcing functions.

The Heaviside Step Function Using the Heaviside function allows you to model delayed and piecewise-defined forcing functions. You can use Heaviside with dsolve to find both symbolic and numeric solutions.

```
> eq := diff(y(t),t) = -y(t)*Heaviside(t-1);
```

$$eq := \frac{d}{dt}\,y(t) = -y(t)\,\text{Heaviside}(t-1)$$

```
> ini := y(0) = 3;
```

$$ini := y(0) = 3$$

```
> dsolve({eq, ini}, {y(t)});
```

$$y(t) = 3\,e^{((-t+1)\,\text{Heaviside}(t-1))}$$

Convert the solution to a function that can be plotted.

```
> rhs( % );
```

$$3\,e^{((-t+1)\,\text{Heaviside}(t-1))}$$

```
> f := unapply(%, t);
```

$$f := t \rightarrow 3\,e^{((-t+1)\,\text{Heaviside}(t-1))}$$

```
> plot(f, 0..4);
```

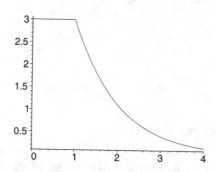

Solve the same equation numerically.

```
> sol1 := dsolve({eq, ini}, {y(t)}, type=numeric);
```

$$sol1 := \mathbf{proc}(x\_rkf45) \ldots \mathbf{end\ proc}$$

You can use the `odeplot` command from the `plots` package to plot the solution.

```
> with(plots):
```

```
> odeplot( sol1, [t, y(t)], 0..4 );
```

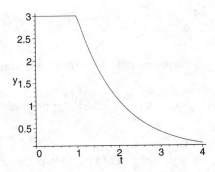

The Dirac Delta Function   You can use the Dirac delta function in a manner similar to the Heaviside function above to produce impulsive forcing functions.

```
> eq := diff(y(t),t) = -y(t)*Dirac(t-1);
```

$$eq := \frac{d}{dt}\,y(t) = -y(t)\,\mathrm{Dirac}(t-1)$$

```
> ini := y(0) = 3;
```

$$ini := y(0) = 3$$

```
> dsolve({eq, ini}, {y(t)});
```

$$y(t) = 3\,e^{(-\mathrm{Heaviside}(t-1))}$$

Convert the solution to a function that can be plotted.

```
> f := unapply( rhs( % ), t );
```

$$f := t \to 3\,e^{(-\text{Heaviside}(t-1))}$$

```
> plot( f, 0..4 );
```

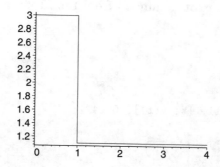

However, the numeric solution does not see the nonzero value of `Dirac(0)`.

```
> sol2 := dsolve({eq, ini}, {y(t)}, type=numeric);
```

$$sol2 := \mathbf{proc}(x\_rkf45) \ldots \mathbf{end\ proc}$$

Again, use odeplot from plots to plot the numeric solution.

```
> with(plots, odeplot);
```

$$[odeplot]$$

```
> odeplot( sol2, [t,y(t)], 0..4 );
```

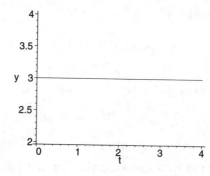

Piecewise Functions   The `piecewise` command allows you to construct complicated forcing functions by approximating sections of it with analytic functions, and then taking the approximations together to represent the whole function. First, look at the behavior of `piecewise`.

```
> f:=  x -> piecewise(1<=x and x<2, 1, 0);
```

$$f := x \rightarrow \text{piecewise}(1 \le x \textbf{ and } x < 2, 1, 0)$$

```
> f(x);
```

$$\begin{cases} 1, & \text{if }, 1 - x \le 0 \text{ and } x - 2 < 0; \\ 0, & \text{otherwise.} \end{cases}$$

Note that the order of the conditionals is important. The first conditional that returns **true** causes the function to return a value.

```
> plot(f, 0..3);
```

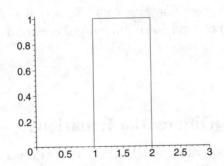

Thus, you can use this piecewise function as a forcing function.

```
> eq := diff(y(t),t) = 1-y(t)*f(t);
```

$$eq := \frac{\partial}{\partial t} y(t) = 1 - y(t) \left(\begin{cases} 1, & \text{if } 1 - t \le 0 \text{ and } t - 2 < 0; \\ 0, & \text{otherwise.} \end{cases} \right)$$

```
> ini := y(0)=3;
```

$$ini := y(0) = 3$$

```
> sol3 := dsolve({eq, ini}, {y(t)}, type=numeric);
```

$$sol3 := \mathbf{proc}(x\_rkf45) \ldots \mathbf{end\ proc}$$

Again, use the `odeplot` command in the `plots` package to plot the result.

```
> with(plots, odeplot):
> odeplot( sol3, [t, y(t)], 0..4 );
```

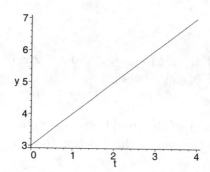

The `DEtools` package contains commands that can help you investigate, manipulate, plot, and solve differential equations. For details, refer to `?DEtools`.

6.3   Partial Differential Equations

Partial differential equations (PDEs) are in general very difficult to solve. Maple provides a number of commands for solving, manipulating, and plotting PDEs. Some of these commands are in the standard library, but most of them reside in the `PDEtools` package.

The `pdsolve` Command

The `pdsolve` command can solve many partial differential equations. This is the basic syntax of the `pdsolve` command.

```
pdsolve( pde, var )
```

Here *pde* is the partial differential equation and *var* is the variable for which you want Maple to solve.

The following is the one-dimensional wave equation.

```
> wave := diff(u(x,t), t,t) - c^2 * diff(u(x,t), x,x);
```

$$wave := (\frac{\partial^2}{\partial t^2} \, u(x, \, t)) - c^2 \, (\frac{\partial^2}{\partial x^2} \, u(x, \, t))$$

You want to solve for u(x,t). First load the PDEtools package.

```
> with(PDEtools):
> sol := pdsolve( wave, u(x,t) );
```

$$sol := u(x, \, t) = \_F1(ct + x) + \_F2(ct - x)$$

Note the solution is in terms of two arbitrary functions, _F1 and _F2. To plot the solution you need a particular set of functions.

```
> f1 := xi -> exp(-xi^2);
```

$$f1 := \xi \rightarrow e^{(-\xi^2)}$$

```
> f2 := xi -> piecewise(-1/2<xi and xi<1/2, 1, 0);
```

$$f2 := \xi \rightarrow \text{piecewise}(\frac{-1}{2} < \xi \text{ and } \xi < \frac{1}{2}, \, 1, \, 0)$$

Substitute these functions into the solution.

```
> eval( sol, {_F1=f1, _F2=f2, c=1} );
```

$$u(x, \, t) = e^{(-(t+x)^2)} + \left(\begin{cases} 1 & -t + x < \frac{1}{2} \text{ and } t - x < \frac{1}{2} \\ 0 & otherwise \end{cases} \right)$$

You can use the **rhs** command to select the solution.

```
> rhs(%);
```

$$e^{(-(t+x)^2)} + \left(\begin{cases} 1 & -t + x < \frac{1}{2} \text{ and } t - x < \frac{1}{2} \\ 0 & otherwise \end{cases} \right)$$

The **unapply** command converts the expression to a function.

```
> f := unapply(%, x,t);
```

$$f := (x,\, t) \rightarrow$$

$$e^{(-(t+x)^2)} + \mathrm{piecewise}\left(-t + x < \frac{1}{2} \text{ and } t - x < \frac{1}{2},\, 1,\, 0\right)$$

Now you can plot the solution.

```
> plot3d( f, -8..8, 0..5, grid=[40,40] );
```

Changing the Dependent Variable in a PDE

The following is the one-dimensional heat equation.

```
> heat := diff(u(x,t),t) - k*diff(u(x,t), x,x) = 0;
```

$$heat := \left(\frac{\partial}{\partial t}\,\mathrm{u}(x,\, t)\right) - k\left(\frac{\partial^2}{\partial x^2}\,\mathrm{u}(x,\, t)\right) = 0$$

Try to find a solution of the form $X(x)T(t)$ to this equation. Use the aptly named HINT option of pdsolve to suggest a course of action.

```
> pdsolve( heat, u(x,t), HINT=X(x)*T(t));
```

$$(\mathrm{u}(x,\, t) = \mathrm{X}(x)\,\mathrm{T}(t))\ \&\text{where}$$

$$\left[\left\{\tfrac{d}{dt}\,\mathrm{T}(t) = k\,\_c_1\,\mathrm{T}(t),\ \tfrac{d^2}{dx^2}\,\mathrm{X}(x) = \_c_1\,\mathrm{X}(x)\right\}\right]$$

The result here is correct, but difficult to read.

Alternatively, you can tell pdsolve to use separation of variables (as a product, '*') and then solve the resulting ODEs (using the 'build' option).

```
> sol := pdsolve(heat, u(x,t), HINT='*', 'build');
```

$$sol := u(x,\,t) = e^{(\sqrt{-c_1}\,x)}\,\_C3\,e^{(k\,\_c_1\,t)}\,\_C1 + \frac{\_C3\,e^{(k\,\_c_1\,t)}\,\_C2}{e^{(\sqrt{-c_1}\,x)}}$$

Evaluate the solution at specific values for the constants.

```
> S := eval( rhs(sol), {_C3=1, _C1=1, _C2=1, k=1, _c[1]=1} );
```

$$S := e^x\,e^t + \frac{e^t}{e^x}$$

You can plot the solution.

```
> plot3d( S, x=-5..5, t=0..5 );
```

Checking the solution by evaluation with the original equation is a good idea.

```
> eval( heat, u(x,t)=rhs(sol) );
```

$$\%1\,\_C3\,k\,\_c_1\,e^{(k\,\_c_1\,t)}\,\_C1 + \frac{\_C3\,k\,\_c_1\,e^{(k\,\_c_1\,t)}\,\_C2}{\%1}$$
$$- k\left(\_c_1\,\%1\,\_C3\,e^{(k\,\_c_1\,t)}\,\_C1 + \frac{\_C3\,e^{(k\,\_c_1\,t)}\,\_C2\,\_c_1}{\%1}\right) = 0$$
$$\%1 := e^{(\sqrt{-c_1}\,x)}$$

```
> simplify(%);
```

$$0 = 0$$

Plotting Partial Differential Equations

The solutions to many PDEs can be plotted with the PDEplot command found in the PDEtools package.

```
> with(PDEtools):
```

You can use the PDEplot command with the following syntax.

```
PDEplot( pde, var, ini, s=range )
```

Here *pde* is the PDE, *var* is the dependent variable, *ini* is a parametric curve in three-dimensional space with parameter *s*, and *range* is the range of *s*.

Consider this partial differential equation.

```
> pde := diff(u(x,y), x) + cos(2*x) * diff(u(x,y), y) = -sin(y);
```

$$pde := (\frac{\partial}{\partial x} \operatorname{u}(x, y)) + \cos(2\,x)\,(\frac{\partial}{\partial y} \operatorname{u}(x, y)) = -\sin(y)$$

Use the curve given by $z = 1 + y^2$ as an initial condition, that is, $x = 0$, $y = s$, and $z = 1 + s^2$.

```
> ini := [0, s, 1+s^2];
```

$$ini := [0, s, 1 + s^2]$$

PDEplot draws the initial-condition curve and the solution surface.

```
> PDEplot( pde, u(x,y), ini, s=-2..2 );
```

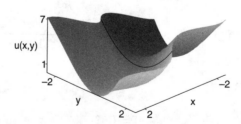

To draw the surface, Maple calculates these base characteristic curves. The initial-condition curve is easier to see here than in the previous plot.

```
> PDEplot( pde, u(x,y), ini, s=-2..2, basechar=only );
```

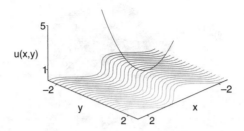

The `basechar=true` option tells `PDEplot` to draw both the characteristic curves and the surface, as well as the initial-condition curve which is always present.

```
> PDEplot( pde, u(x,y), ini, s=-2..2, basechar=true );
```

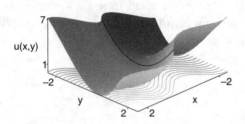

Many `plot3d` options are also available. Refer to `?plot3d,options`. The `initcolor` option sets the color of the initial value curve.

```
> PDEplot( pde, u(x,y), ini, s=-2..2,
>     basechar=true, initcolor=white,
>     style=patchcontour, contours=20,
>     orientation=[-43,45] );
```

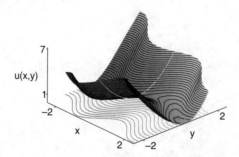

6.4   Conclusion

This chapter has demonstrated how Maple can be used to aid in the investigation and solution of problems using calculus. You have seen how Maple can visually represent concepts, such as the derivative and the Riemann integral; help analyze the error term in a Taylor approximation; and manipulate and solve ordinary and partial differential equations, numerically as well as symbolically.

7   Input and Output

You can do much of your work directly within Maple's worksheets. You can perform calculations, plot functions, and document the results. However, at some point you may need to import data or export results to a file to interact with another person or piece of software. The data could be measurements from scientific experiments or numbers generated by other programs. Once you import the data into Maple, you can use Maple's plotting capabilities to visualize the results, and its algebraic capabilities to construct or investigate an associated mathematical model.

Maple provides a number of convenient ways to both import and export raw numerical data and graphics. It presents individual algebraic and numeric results in formats suitable for use in FORTRAN, C, or the mathematical typesetting system LaTeX. You can even export the entire worksheet as a text file (for inclusion in electronic mail), a LaTeX document, HTML, RTF, or XML. You can cut and paste results, and export either single expressions or entire worksheets.

This chapter discusses the most common aspects of exporting and importing information to and from files. It introduces how Maple interacts with the file system on your computer, and how Maple can begin interacting with other software.

7.1   Reading Files

The two most common reasons to read files are to obtain data and to retrieve Maple commands stored in a text file.

The first case is often concerned with data generated from an experiment. You can store numbers separated by white space and line breaks in a text file, then read them into Maple for study. You can most easily accomplish these operations by using Maple's `ExportMatrix` and `ImportMatrix` commands, respectively.

The second case concerns reading commands from a text file. Perhaps you have received a worksheet in text format, or written a Maple procedure by using your favorite text editor and stored it in a text file. You can cut and paste commands into Maple or you can use the **read** command. This section discusses the latter option.

Reading Columns of Numbers from a File

Maple is very good at manipulating data. If you generate data outside Maple, you must read it into Maple before you can manipulate it. Often such external data is in the form of columns of numbers in a text file. The file **data.txt** below is an example.

```
0 1              0
1 .5403023059 .8414709848
2 -.4161468365 .9092974268
3 -.9899924966 .1411200081
4 -.6536436209 -.7568024953
5 .2836621855 -.9589242747
6 .9601702867 -.2794154982
```

The `ImportMatrix` command reads columns of numbers. Use `ImportMatrix` as follows.

```
ImportMatrix( "filename", delimiter=string )
```

Here, *filename* is the name of the file that you want `ImportMatrix` to read, and *string* is the character that separates the entries in the file. The default value of *string* is a tab, represented by using "\t". In **data.txt**, the entries are separated by spaces, so the value of *string* is " ".

```
> L := ImportMatrix( "data.txt", delimiter="\t" );
```

$$
L := \begin{bmatrix}
0 & 1 & 0 \\
1 & 0.5403023059 & 0.8414709848 \\
2 & -0.4161468365 & 0.9092974268 \\
3 & -0.9899924966 & 0.1411200081 \\
4 & -0.6536436209 & -0.7568024953 \\
5 & 0.2836621855 & -0.9589242747 \\
6 & 0.9601702867 & -0.2794154982
\end{bmatrix}
$$

For example, you can plot the third column against the first. Use the **convert** command to select the first and the third entries in each column.

```
> convert( L[[1..-1],[1,3]], listlist );
```

$$[[0, 0], [1, 0.8414709848], [2, 0.9092974268],$$
$$[3, 0.1411200081], [4, -0.7568024953],$$
$$[5, -0.9589242747], [6, -0.2794154982]]$$

The `plot` command can plot lists directly.

```
> plot(%);
```

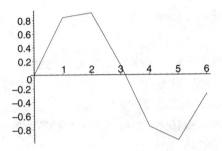

To select the second column of numbers, you can use the fact that `L[5,2]` is the second number in the fifth sublist,

```
> L[5,2];
```

$$-0.6536436209$$

So, you need the following data.

```
> L[ 1..-1, 2 ];
```

$$\begin{bmatrix} 1 \\ 0.5403023059 \\ -0.4161468365 \\ -0.9899924966 \\ -0.6536436209 \\ 0.2836621855 \\ 0.9601702867 \end{bmatrix}$$

Convert this data to a list, and then find the mean.

```
> convert(L[1..-1,2],list);
```

$$[1, 0.5403023059, -0.4161468365, -0.9899924966,$$
$$-0.6536436209, 0.2836621855, 0.9601702867]$$

```
> stats[describe,mean](%) ;
```

$$0.1034788321$$

You can also perform calculations on your matrix L using the LinearAlgebra package.

```
> LinearAlgebra[Transpose](L) . L;
```

$$[91., 1.30278930720000119, -6.41489848119999984]$$
$$[1.30278930720000119, 3.87483111270157598,$$
$$-0.109078174475632172]$$
$$[-6.41489848119999984, -0.109078174475632172,$$
$$3.12516888746710864]$$

For more information regarding options for use with ImportMatrix, refer to ?ImportMatrix.

Reading Commands from a File

Some Maple users find it convenient to write Maple programs in a text file with their favorite text editor, and then import the file into Maple. You can paste the commands from the text file into your worksheet or you can use the read command.

When you read a file with the read command, Maple treats each line in the file as a command. Maple executes the commands and displays the results in your worksheet but it does *not*, by default, place the commands from the file in your worksheet. Use the read command with the following syntax.

```
read "filename";
```

For example, the file ks.tst contains the following Maple commands.

```
S := n -> sum( binomial(n, beta)
    * ( (2*beta)!/2^beta - beta!*beta ), beta=1..n );
S( 19 );
```

When you read the file, Maple displays the results but not the commands.

```
> read "ks.tst";
```

$$S := n \rightarrow \sum_{\beta=1}^{n} \text{binomial}(n, \beta)\,(\frac{(2\,\beta)!}{2^{\beta}} - \beta!\,\beta)$$

$$10249373616666445980711143287693179982974$$

If you set the `interface` variable `echo` to 2, Maple inserts the commands from the file into your worksheet.

```
> interface( echo=2 );
> read "ks.tst";

> S := n -> sum( binomial(n, beta)
>     * ( (2*beta)!/2^beta - beta!*beta ), beta=1..n );
```

$$S := n \rightarrow \sum_{\beta=1}^{n} \text{binomial}(n, \beta)\,(\frac{(2\,\beta)!}{2^{\beta}} - \beta!\,\beta)$$

```
> S( 19 );
```

$$10249373616666445980711143287693179982974$$

The **read** command can also read files in Maple's internal format. See section 7.2.

7.2   Writing Data to a File

After using Maple to perform a calculation, you may want to save the result in a file. You can then process the result later, either with Maple or with another program.

Writing Columns of Numerical Data to a File

If the result of a Maple calculation is a long list or a large array of numbers, you can convert it to a Matrix and write the numbers to a file in a structured manner. The **ExportMatrix** command writes columns of numerical data to a file, allowing you to import the numbers into another program. You can use the **ExportMatrix** command with the following syntax.

```
ExportMatrix( "filename", data )
```

Here, *filename* is the string containing the name of the file to which **ExportMatrix** writes the data, and *data* is a Matrix. Note that any list, vector, list of lists, or table-based matrix can be converted to a Matrix by using the Matrix constructor. For more information, refer to *?Matrix*.

> L:=LinearAlgebra[RandomMatrix](5);

$$L := \begin{bmatrix} -66 & -65 & 20 & -90 & 30 \\ 55 & 5 & -7 & -21 & 62 \\ 68 & 66 & 16 & -56 & -79 \\ 26 & -36 & -34 & -8 & -71 \\ 13 & -41 & -62 & -50 & 28 \end{bmatrix}$$

> ExportMatrix("matrixdata.txt", L):

If the data is a Vector or any object that can be converted to type Vector, then **ExportVector** can be used. Lists and table-based vectors can be converted by using the Vector constructor. For more information, refer to *?Vector*.

> L := [3, 3.1415, -65, 0];

$$L := [3, 3.1415, -65, 0]$$

> V := Vector(L);

$$V := \begin{bmatrix} 3 \\ 3.1415 \\ -65 \\ 0 \end{bmatrix}$$

> ExportVector("vectordata.txt", V):

You can extend these routines so that they write more complicated data, such as complex numbers or symbolic expressions. For more information, refer to *?ExportMatrix* and *?ExportVector*.

Saving Expressions in Maple's Internal Format

If you construct a complicated expression or procedure, you may want to save it for future use in Maple. If you save the expression or procedure in Maple's internal format, then Maple can retrieve it efficiently. You can accomplish this by using the **save** command to write the expression to a file whose name ends with the characters ".m". Use the **save** command with the following syntax.

```
save nameseq, "filename.m";
```

Here *nameseq* is a sequence of names; you can save only named objects. The **save** command saves the objects in *filename*.m. The .m indicates that **save** will write the file using Maple's internal format.

Consider the following.

```
> qbinomial := (n,k) -> product(1-q^i, i=n-k+1..n) /
>                       product(1-q^i, i=1..k );
```

$$qbinomial := (n,\, k) \rightarrow \frac{\displaystyle\prod_{i=n-k+1}^{n} (1 - q^i)}{\displaystyle\prod_{i=1}^{k} (1 - q^i)}$$

```
> expr := qbinomial(10, 4);
```

$$expr := \frac{(1 - q^7)\,(1 - q^8)\,(1 - q^9)\,(1 - q^{10})}{(1 - q)\,(1 - q^2)\,(1 - q^3)\,(1 - q^4)}$$

```
> nexpr := normal( expr );
```

$$nexpr := (q^6 + q^5 + q^4 + q^3 + q^2 + q + 1)\,(q^4 + 1)\,(q^6 + q^3 + 1)$$
$$(q^8 + q^6 + q^4 + q^2 + 1)$$

You can now save these expressions to the file **qbinom.m**.

```
> save qbinomial, expr, nexpr, "qbinom.m";
```

The **restart** command clears the three expressions from memory. Thus **expr** evaluates to its own name below.

```
> restart:
> expr;
```

$$expr$$

Use the **read** command to retrieve the expressions that you saved in qbinom.m.

```
> read "qbinom.m";
```

Now **expr** has its value again.

```
> expr;
```

$$\frac{(1-q^7)\,(1-q^8)\,(1-q^9)\,(1-q^{10})}{(1-q)\,(1-q^2)\,(1-q^3)\,(1-q^4)}$$

For more information on the **read** command, see section 7.1.

Converting to LATEX Format

TEX is a program for typesetting mathematics, and LATEX is a macro package for TEX. The **latex** command converts Maple expressions to LATEX format. You can perform conversion to LATEX by using the **latex** command. Thus, you can use Maple to solve a problem, then convert the result to LATEX code that can be included in a LATEX document. Use the **latex** command in the following manner.

```
latex( expr, "filename" )
```

The *expr* can be any mathematical expression. Maple-specific expressions, such as procedures, are not translatable. The *filename* is optional, and specifies that Maple writes the translated output to the file you specified. If you do not specify a *filename*, Maple writes the output to the **default** output stream (your session).

The **latex** command writes the LATEX code corresponding to the Maple expression *expr* to the file *filename*. If *filename* exists, **latex** overwrites it. If you omit *filename*, **latex** prints the LATEX code on the screen. You can cut and paste from the output into your LATEX document.

```
> latex( a/b );
```

```
{\frac {a}{b}}
```

```
> latex( Limit( int(f(x), x=-n..n), n=infinity ) );
```

```
\lim _{n\rightarrow \infty }\int _{-n}^{n}\!f
\left( x \right) {dx}
```

The `latex` command produces code suitable for LATEX's math mode. However, it does not produce the command for entering and leaving math mode, and it does not attempt any line breaking or alignment.

The `latex` command can translate most types of mathematical expressions, including integrals, limits, sums, products, and matrices. You can expand the capabilities of `latex` by defining procedures with names of the form `latex/functionname`. Such a procedure formats calls to the function called *functionname*. You should produce the output of such formatting functions with the `printf` command. The `latex` command uses the `writeto` command to redirect the output when you specify a *filename*.

The `latex` command does not generate the commands that LATEX requires to put the typesetting system into mathematics mode ($...$, for example).

The following example shows the generation of LATEX for an equation for an integral and its value. Notice the use of `Int`, the inert form of `int`, to prevent evaluation of the left hand side of the equation that Maple is formatting.

```
> Int(1/(x^4+1),x) = int(1/(x^4+1),x);
```

$$\int \frac{1}{x^4+1}\, dx = \frac{1}{8}\,\sqrt{2}\ln(\frac{x^2+x\sqrt{2}+1}{x^2-x\sqrt{2}+1}) + \frac{1}{4}\,\sqrt{2}\arctan(x\sqrt{2}+1)$$
$$+ \frac{1}{4}\,\sqrt{2}\arctan(x\sqrt{2}-1)$$

```
> latex(%);
```

```
\int \! \left( {x}^{4}+1 \right) ^{-1}{dx}=1/8
\,\sqrt {2}\ln  \left( {\frac {{x}^{2}+x\sqrt
{2}+1}{{x}^{2}-x\sqrt {2}+1}} \right) +1/4\,
\sqrt {2}\arctan \left( x\sqrt {2}+1 \right) +
1/4\,\sqrt {2}\arctan \left( x\sqrt {2}-1
\right)
```

Section 7.3 describes how you can save an entire worksheet in LATEX format.

7.3   Exporting Whole Worksheets

You can save your worksheets by choosing **Save** or **Save As** from the **File** menu. However, you can also export a worksheet in six other formats: plain text, Maple text, LATEX, HTML, HTML with MathML, RTF, and XML, by choosing **Export As** from the **File** menu. This allows you to process a worksheet outside Maple.

Plain Text

To save a worksheet as plain text, select **Export As** from the **File** menu, then **Plain Text**. In this case, Maple precedes input with a greater-than sign and a space (>). Maple uses character-based typesetting for special symbols like integral signs and exponents, but you cannot export graphics as text. The following is a portion of a Maple worksheet exported in plain text format.

```
An Indefinite Integral
by Jane Maplefan
Calculation
Look at the integral Int(x^2*sin(x-a),x);. Notice that its
integrand, x^2*sin(x-a);, depends on the parameter a;.
Give the integral a name so that you can refer to it later.
> expr := Int(x^2 * sin(x-a), x);
```

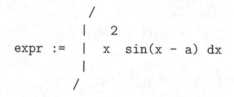

```
                     /
                     |    2
         expr :=     |   x  sin(x - a) dx
                     |
                     /
```

```
The value of the integral is an anti-derivative of the
integrand.
> answer := value( % );
```

Maple Text

Maple text is specially marked text that retains the worksheet's distinction between text, Maple input, and Maple output. Thus, you can export a worksheet as Maple text, send the text file by electronic mail, and the recipient can import the Maple text into a Maple session and regenerate most of the structure of your original worksheet. When reading or pasting Maple text, Maple treats each line that begins with a Maple prompt and a space (>) as Maple input, each line that begins with a hash mark and a space (#) as text, and ignores all other lines.

To export an entire worksheet as Maple text, select **Export As** from the **File** menu, then **Maple Text**. The following is a portion of a Maple worksheet exported as Maple text.

```
# An Indefinite Integral
# by Jane Maplefan
# Calculation
# Look at the integral Int(x^2*sin(x-a),x);. Notice that its
# integrand, x^2*sin(x-a);, depends on the parameter a;.
# Give the integral a name so that you can refer to it later.
> expr := Int(x^2 * sin(x-a), x);


                           /
                           |   2
              expr :=      |  x   sin(x - a) dx
                           |
                           /


# The value of the integral is an anti-derivative of the
# integrand.
> answer := value( % );
```

To open a worksheet in Maple text format as the one above, select **Open** from the **File** menu. In the dialog box that appears, select **Maple Text** from the drop-down list of file types. Double-click the desired file, then select **Maple Text** in the dialog box that appears.

You can also copy and paste Maple text by using the **Edit** menu. If you copy a part of your worksheet as Maple text and paste it into another application, then the pasted text appears as Maple text. Similarly, if you paste Maple text into your worksheet by using **Paste Maple Text** from the **Edit** menu, then Maple retains the structure of the Maple text. In contrast, if you use ordinary paste, Maple does not retain its structure. If you paste into an input region, Maple interprets the pasted section as input. If you paste into a text region, Maple interprets the pasted section as text.

LaTeX

To export a Maple worksheet in LaTeX format, select **Export As** from the **File** menu, then **LaTeX**. The `.tex` file that Maple generates is ready for processing by LaTeX. All distributions of Maple include the necessary style files.

If your worksheet contains embedded graphics, then Maple generates PostScript files corresponding to the graphics and inserts the LaTeX code to include these PostScript files in your LaTeX document.

The following is a portion of a Maple worksheet exported as LaTeX.

```
%% Created by Maple 7.00 (IBM INTEL NT)
%% Source Worksheet: tut1.mws
%% Generated: Wed Apr 11 12:23:32 2001
\documentclass{article}
\usepackage{maple2e}
\DefineParaStyle{Author}
\DefineParaStyle{Heading 1}
\DefineParaStyle{Maple Output}
\DefineParaStyle{Maple Plot}
\DefineParaStyle{Title}
\DefineCharStyle{2D Comment}
\DefineCharStyle{2D Math}
\DefineCharStyle{2D Output}
\DefineCharStyle{Hyperlink}
\begin{document}
\begin{maplegroup}
\begin{Title}
An Indefinite Integral
\end{Title}

\begin{Author}
by Jane Maplefan
\end{Author}

\end{maplegroup}

\section{Calculation}

Look at the integral
\mapleinline{inert}{2d}{Int(x^2*sin(x-a),x);}{%
$\int x^{2}\,\mathrm{sin}(x - a)\,dx$%
}. Notice that its integrand,
\mapleinline{inert}{2d}{x^2*sin(x-a);}{%
$x^{2}\,\mathrm{sin}(x - a)$%
}, depends on the parameter
\mapleinline{inert}{2d}{a;}{%
```

```
$a$%
}.
```

The LATEX style files assume that you are printing the `.tex` file using the **dvips** printer driver. You can change this default by specifying an option to the `\usepackage` LATEX command in the preamble of your `.tex` file.

Section 7.4 describes how to save graphics directly. You can include such graphics files in your LATEX document by using the `\mapleplot` LATEX command.

HTML and HTML with MathML

To export a Maple worksheet in HTML (HyperText Markup Language) format, select **Export As** from the **File** menu, then **HTML**. The `.html` file that Maple generates can be loaded into any HTML browser. To export a Maple worksheet in HTML with MathML (Mathematical Markup Language) format, select **Export As** from the **File** menu, then **HTML with MathML**. MathML is the Internet standard, sanctioned by the World Wide Web Consortium (W3C), for the communication of structured mathematical formulae between applications. For more information about MathML, refer to the help page `?MathML`.

Maple generates `.gif` files to represent plots and animations in your worksheet. Maple converts formatted mathematical output to MathML or `.gif` file format for HTML with MathML or HTML exports, respectively.

The following is a Maple worksheet exported as HTML. Notice that other HTML documents (including a table of contents), which were created by the export process, are called within it.

```
<html>
<head>
<title>tut1.htm</title>
<!-- Created by Maple 7.00, IBM INTEL NT -->
</head>
<basefont size=3>
<frameset cols="25%,*">
  <frame src="tut1TOC.htm" name="TableOfContents">
  <frame src="tut11.htm" name="Content">
<noframes>
Sorry, this document requires that your browser support
frames.
<a href="tut11.htm" target="Content">This link</a>
will take you to a non-frames presentation of the document.
```

```
</noframes>
</frameset>
</basefont>
</html>
```

The following is a portion of the tut11.htm file called in the above file.

```
<b><font color=#000000 size=5>Calculation</font></b>
</p>
<p align=left>
<font color=#000000>Look at the integral </font>
<img src="tut11.gif" width=120 height=60 alt="[Maple Math]"
align=middle>
<font color=#000000>. Notice that its integrand, </font>
<img src="tut12.gif" width=89 height=50 alt="[Maple Math]"
align=middle>
<font color=#000000>, depends on the parameter </font>
<img src="tut13.gif" width=13 height=32 alt="[Maple Math]"
align=middle>
<font color=#000000>.</font>
</p>
<p align=left>
<font color=#000000>Give the integral a name so that you
can refer to it later.</font>
</p>
<p align=left><a name="expr command">
<tt>&gt; </tt>
<b><font color=#FF0000>expr := Int(x^2 * sin(x-a),
x);</font></b>
</p>
<p align=center>
<img src="tut14.gif" width=169 height=49 alt="[Maple Math]">
</p>
<p align=left>
<font color=#000000>The value of the integral is </font>
<a href="tut4.html" target="_top">an anti-derivative</a>
<font color=#000000> of the integrand.</font>
</p>
```

RTF

To export a Maple worksheet in RTF (Rich Text Format), select **Export As** from the **File** menu, then **RTF**. The `.rtf` file that Maple generates can be loaded into any word processor that supports RTF. Maple embeds plots and formatted math in the file as bitmaps wrapped in Windows Metafiles. Spreadsheets are not fully exported, but visible cells and column and row headers are exported.

The following is a portion of a Maple worksheet exported as RTF.

```
{\rtf1\ansi\ansicpg1252\deff0\deflang1033
{\fonttbl
{\f0 Times New Roman}
{\f1 Symbol}
{\f2 Courier New}
}
{\colortbl
\red205\green205\blue205;
\red255\green0\blue0;
\red0\green0\blue0;
\red0\green0\blue255;
}
{\stylesheet
{\s0 \widctlpar}
{\s1\qr footer_header}
{\*\cs12\f2\fs24\cf1\i0 \b \ul0 \additive Maple Input}
{\*\cs13\f0\fs24\cf2\i0 \b0 \ul0 \additive 2D Comment}
{\*\cs14\f0\fs24\cf1\i0 \b0 \ul0 \additive 2D Input}
{\*\cs15\f0\fs24\cf3\i0 \b0 \ul0 \additive 2D Output}
```

XML

To export a Maple worksheet in XML (Extensible Markup Language), select **Export As** from the **File** menu, then **XML**. The `.xml` file that Maple generates can be loaded as a worksheet. XML documents are loaded by choosing **Open** from the **File** menu.

The following is a excerpt of a Maple worksheet exported as XML.

```
<section><exchange><para pstyle='Normal' prompt='> '><mapletext
maple-input='true' cstyle='Maple Input'>a;</mapletext></para>
</exchange></section>
```

7.4   Printing Graphics

On most platforms, Maple by default displays graphics directly in the worksheet—as *inline plots*. You can use the `plotsetup` command to change this behavior. The following command instructs Maple to display graphics in separate windows on your screen.

```
> plotsetup(window);
```

With your plot in a separate window, you can print it through the **File** menu as you would print any other worksheet.

The `plotsetup` command has the following general syntax.

```
plotsetup( DeviceType, plotoutput="filename",
          plotoption="options" )
```

Here, *DeviceType* is the graphics device that Maple should use, *filename* is the name of the output file, and *options* is a string of options that the graphics driver recognizes.

The following command instructs Maple to send graphics in PostScript format to the file `myplot.ps`.

```
> plotsetup( postscript, plotoutput="myplot.ps" );
```

The plot that the following `plot` command generates does not appear on the screen but, instead, goes to the file `myplot.ps`.

```
> plot( sin(x^2), x=-4..4 );
```

Maple can also generate graphics in a form suited to an HP LaserJet printer. Maple sends the graph that the following `plot3d` command generates to the file `myplot.hp`.

```
> plotsetup( hpgl, plotoutput="myplot.hp",
>           plotoptions=laserjet );
> plot3d( tan(x*sin(y)), x=-Pi/3..Pi/3, y=-Pi..Pi);
```

If you want to print more than one plot, you must change the `plotoutput` option between each plot. Otherwise, the new plot overwrites the previous one.

```
> plotsetup( plotoutput="myplot2.hp" );
> plot( exp@sin, 0..10 );
```

When you are done exporting graphics, you must tell Maple to send future graphics to your worksheet again.

```
> plotsetup( inline );
```

For a description of the plotting devices supported in Maple, refer to `?plot,device`.

7.5 Conclusion

In this chapter, you have seen a number of Maple's elementary input and output facilities: how to print graphics, how to save and retrieve individual Maple expressions, how to read and write numerical data, and how to export a Maple worksheet as a LaTeX or HTML document.

In addition, Maple has many low-level input and output commands, such as `fprintf`, `fscanf`, `writeline`, `readbytes`, `fopen`, and `fclose`. Refer to the corresponding help pages for details.

The help pages are Maple's interactive reference manual. They are always at your fingertips when you are using Maple. Like a traditional reference manual, use them by studying the index, or by searching through them. In particular, the complete text search facility provides a method of searching for information, superior to a traditional index. In addition, hyperlinks make it easy for you to check related topics.

This book aims to supply you with a good base of knowledge from which to further explore Maple. In this role, it focuses on the interactive use of Maple. Of course, Maple is a complete language, and provides complete facilities for programming. In fact, the majority of Maple's commands are coded in the Maple language, as this high-level, mathematically oriented language is far superior to traditional computer languages for such tasks. The *Maple Introductory Programming Guide* introduces you to programming in Maple.

8   Maplets

By using the `Maplets` package, you can create windows, dialogs, and other visual interfaces that interact with a user to provide the power of Maple.

Users can perform calculations, or plot functions without using the worksheet interface.

This chapter is intended primarily for maplet users. Some information may be helpful to maplet authors.

8.1   Example Maplet

You can create an interface that requests user input, for example, an integration maplet can be designed to have the following appearance and components.

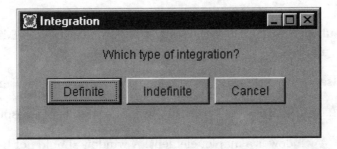

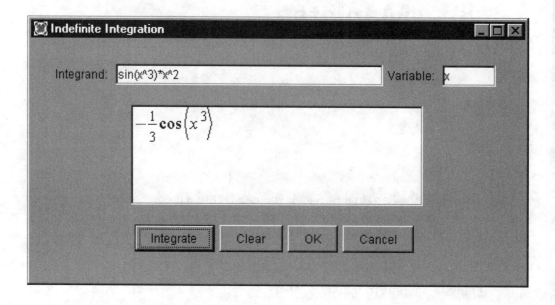

8.2 Terminology

Maplet   A maplet is a collection of elements, including, but not limited to, windows, their associated layouts, dialogs, and actions. A maplet differs from windows and dialogs in that a maplet contains windows and dialogs.

Maplet Author   A maplet author is a programmer who uses Maple code to write a maplet.

Maplet User   A maple user is someone who interacts with a maplet.

Layout   Layout defines how elements within a maplet are displayed.

Window   A window is a maplet element. A window should not be thought of as a maplet, but rather as one element within a maplet. A maplet can contain more than one window. Each window can contain many elements that control the layout and function of the window.

Dialog   A dialog is a maplet element. Unlike a window, which can contain elements, for example, buttons or layout elements, a dialog element has a predefined structure. An author can specify options for a dialog, but cannot add elements.

8.3   How to Start the Maplets **Package**

If you receive a Maple worksheet with Maplets code, you must first invoke the Maplets package. Press the ENTER key after these two possible execution groups:

```
> restart:
> with(Maplets[Elements]);
```

Important: You must have Java™ Runtime Environment Version 1.2.2 installed on your local system. If you do not have Java Runtime Environment Version 1.2.2 installed, see your system administrator. If you are running Red Hat Linux 7.0, Java Runtime Environment Version 1.3 is required. If you do not have Java Runtime Environment Version 1.3 installed, see your system administrator.

8.4   How to Invoke a Maplet from the Maple Worksheet

To start a maplet, press the ENTER key after the last colon (:), semicolon (;), or anywhere in an execution group to execute the Maplets code. In the following example, the maplet is written as one execution group. You can press ENTER anywhere in the execution group to execute the code:

```
> mymaplet := Maplet ([
> ["Hello World", Button("OK", Shutdown())]
> ]):
> Maplets[Display](mymaplet);
```

In the following example, the maplet is written as two execution groups. The maplet must be defined before using the Display command.

```
> with(Maplets[Elements]):
> my2maplet := Maplet ([
> ["Hello World #2", Button("OK", Shutdown())]
> ]):
> Maplets[Display](my2maplet);
```

8.5   How to Close a Maplet

If the maplet contains a cancel button, click **Cancel**. Otherwise, click the appropriate Close icon for your platform. For example:

In UNIX:

1. Click the - icon in the upper left corner of the maplet window title bar. A drop-down list box appears.

    Note: The icon varies with window manager.

2. Select Close.

In Windows:

- Click the **X** icon in the upper right corner of the maplet window title bar. The maplet closes.

8.6   How to Work With Maplets and the Maple Window (Modality)

When a maplet is running, the Maple worksheet is inaccessible. If you move the cursor across the worksheet, an icon (clock in UNIX (depending on your window manager), hourglass in Windows) appears, indicating that the worksheet is inaccessible. The maplet must be closed or allowed to complete an action before the Maple worksheet can be accessed.

8.7   How to Activate a Maplet Window

1. Click an input field in the maplet. The input field appears highlighted.

2. Enter the appropriate expression, numbers, or text as required.

8.8   How to Terminate and Restart a Maplet

With long computations, you may wish to stop the computation.

1. To terminate the current maplet process, click the **X** (or appropriate close icon for your platform) that is on the maplet title bar.

2. To restart the terminated maplet, run the maplet by using the lastmaplet tool.

```
> Maplets[Display](lastmaplet);
```

8.9   How to Use Graphical User Interface Shortcuts

Drop-down List Boxes

Some maplets contain drop-down list boxes.

1. Enter the first character of any item in the list. The list automatically moves to an item that begins with the character entered.

2. Continue to enter the character until the desired selection is highlighted.

Note that this shortcut does not apply to editable drop-down lists created with the ComboBox element.

Space Bar and Tab Key

You can use the mouse to click a **Cancel** or **OK** button in a maplet. You can also use the TAB key and SPACE BAR.

1. Using the TAB key, position the cursor at the **Cancel** or **OK** button.

2. Press the SPACE BAR. The command is entered.

8.10 Conclusion

For more information on Maplets, enter ?maplets at the Maple prompt or refer to the *Maple Introductory Programming Guide*, chapter 9.

Index